HUMANISM AND DEMOCRATIC CRITICISM

COLUMBIA THEMES IN PHILOSOPHY
THE COLUMBIA LECTURES ON AMERICAN CULTURE

COLUMBIA THEMES IN PHILOSOPHY

Editor: Akeel Bilgrami, Johnsonian Professor of Philosophy,
Columbia University

Columbia Themes in Philosophy is a new series with a broad
and accommodating thematic reach as well as an ecumenical
approach to the outdated disjunction between analytical and
European philosophy. It is committed to an examination of
key themes in new and startling ways and to the exploration
of new topics in philosophy.

Michael Dummett, *Truth and the Past*

EDWARD W. SAID

HUMANISM AND
DEMOCRATIC CRITICISM

COLUMBIA UNIVERSITY PRESS   NEW YORK

Columbia University Press
Publishers Since 1893
New York   Chichester, West Sussex
Copyright © 2004 Columbia University Press
All rights reserved

Library of Congress Cataloging-in-Publication Data
Said, Edward W.
    Humanism and democratic criticism / Edward W. Said.
      p. cm. — (Columbia themes in philosophy)
    Includes bibliographical references and index.
    ISBN 0–231–12264–0 (cloth : alk. paper)
    1. Humanism—Social aspects—United States. I. Title. II. Series.
  B821.S15   2004
  144—dc22
                                   2003063535

Columbia University Press books are printed on
permanent and durable acid-free paper.
Printed in the United States of America
c 10 9 8 7 6 5 4 3 2 1

For Richard Poirier,
dear friend, great critic, teacher

CONTENTS

BECAUSE OF HIS GREAT POLITICAL COURAGE, BECAUSE HE repeatedly broke his lion's heart in the cause of Palestinian freedom, because so much of his most famous and familiar work is intellectually continuous with those political themes and struggles, and because it is so often expressed in prose that has the voltage of political dramatization, Edward Said's intellectual legacy will be primarily political—not just in the popular imagination, but also perhaps in the eyes of academic research. This is inevitable and it is perhaps how it should be. But the present work, the last completed book he wrote, allows us to situate this legacy in the larger philosophical setting of his humanism—perhaps the only "ism" that, with stubborn ideals, he continued to avow, despite its being made to seem pious and sentimental by the avant-garde developments in the last few decades of literary theory.

This book has grown out of lectures given first at Columbia University in a series established by Jonathan Cole on behalf of Columbia University Press, and it is now published by the press in this volume as part of its Columbia Themes in Philosophy series. Running through the civic passions and the charged impressionism of Said's lectures is a deep and structured argument.

From its earliest classical hints to the most subtle surviving versions of our own time, two elements of broad generality have abided through humanism's diverse doctrinal formulations. They can, in retrospect, be seen as its defining poles. One is its aspiration to find some feature or features that sets what is human apart—apart from both nature, as the natural sciences study it, and apart from what is super-nature and transcendental, as these are pursued by the outreach of theology or absolute metaphysics. The other is the yearning to show regard for *all* that is human, for what is human *wherever* it may be found and however remote it may be from the more vivid presence of the parochial. The dictum "Nothing human is alien to me," still moving despite its great familiarity (and despite the legend about its trivial origin), conveys something of that yearning.

With these poles framing the complex and criss-crossing lines of this book, the contours of its argument come into relief. At one pole, to explore what sets the human apart, Said invokes early on a principle of Vico's, that we know best what we ourselves make and form—history. Self-knowledge thus becomes special, standing apart from other forms of knowledge. And only human beings, so far as we know, are capable of that self-knowledge. At the other pole, to make urgent the Senecan dictum, Said right at the outset plunges into the topical, warning us of the disasters that will follow, and which indeed are already upon us, if we conduct our public lives as intellectuals with an indifference to the concerns and the suffering of people in places remote from our Western, metropolitan sites of self-interest.

Though these may be relatively fixed poles in the highly changeable set of ideas we call "humanistic," these two features are not poles apart. They are not unrelated and contingent elements of humanism. They must be brought together in a coherent view.

To bridge the distance between them, Said develops these starting points of his narrative, first at one pole, by completing Vico's insight with a striking philosophical addition. What Vico brought to light was the specially human ability for self-knowledge and the special character possessed by self-knowledge among all the other forms of knowledge that we have. This special character, which has been developed since his time in such terms as "*Verstehen*," "*Geisteswissenschaften*," or, as we like to say in America, "the social sciences," still gives no particular hint of the role and centrality of the humanities. By itself, it does not quite even give us yet the subject of these lectures, humanism. It is Said's claim that until we supplement self-knowledge with self-criticism, in fact until we understand self-knowledge as being constituted by self-criticism, humanism and its disciplinary manifestations ("the humanities") are still not visible on the horizon. What makes that supplement and that new understanding possible is the study of literature. To put it schematically, the study of literature, that is to say "criticism," Said's own life-long pursuit, when it supplements *self*-knowledge brings to flourishing the truly unique human capacity, the capacity to be *self-critical*.

Turning then to the other pole, how can a concern for *all* that is human be linked, not just contingently but *necessarily*, to this capacity for self-criticism? Why are these not simply two disparate elements in our understanding of humanism? Said's answer is that when criticism at our universities is not parochial, when it studies the traditions and concepts of other cultures, it opens itself up to resources by which it may become *self*-criticism, resources not present while the focus is cozy and insular. The "Other," therefore, is the source and resource for a better, more critical understanding of the "Self." It is important to see, then, that the appeal of the Senecan ideal for Said cannot degenerate into a fetishization of "diversity" for its own sake or into a glib and "correct" embrace of current multiculturalist tendency. It is strictly a step in an argument that starts with Vico and ends with the relevance of humanism in American life and politics. Multi-culturalism has not had a more learned and lofty defense than is offered in this book.

Even put so briefly, the argument is far-going and instruc-tive. By forging a *methodical* link between the two poles of humanism Said identifies, it allows us to resolve, or at any rate make measurable progress in resolving, something that remained unresolved in Vico's own work—the tension between history and agency. Historicism, the doctrine that grew out of Vichian philosophy, has always presented this tension in an especially vexing form. To know ourselves in history is to see ourselves as objects; it is to see ourselves in the third-person mode rather than to deliberate and act as subjects and agents in the first person. And it is the same ten-sion that is echoed in Clifford's criticism of Said's earlier work, *Orientalism*, which Said generously cites at the very beginning—that he cannot reconcile the denial of the human subject and agency, in his appeal to Foucault in that work, with his own humanist intellectual urges. But if the argument I am detecting in lectures is effective, if it allows us the pas-sage from Vico's stress on history to the fully cosmopolitan basis for self-criticism, we would have gone a long way toward easing these tensions. We may now not simply assert, but claim with some right, as Said does, that criticism is two *seemingly* inconsistent things: it is philology, the "history" of words, the "reception" of a tradition, *and*, at the same, time it is a "resistance" to that tradition and the repository of custom that words accumulate.

The argument thus gives humanism rigor and intellectual muscle, as well as a topicality and political relevance, that makes it unrecognizable from the musty doctrine that it had become earlier in the last century—and it gives those disillusioned or just simply bored with that doctrine something more lively and important to turn to than the arid formalisms and relativisms of recent years. For this we must all be most grateful.

AKEEL BILGRAMI

THE THREE MAIN CHAPTERS OF THIS BOOK WERE FIRST GIVEN
as a set of lectures at Columbia University in January 2000, in
an annual series sponsored by the university and Columbia
University Press on aspects of American culture. The original
invitation came from Provost Jonathan Cole, a dear friend
and long-standing colleague at Columbia whose commitment to intellectual standards and free inquiry have helped
make our university such an extraordinary place. In October
and November 2003, I expanded the lectures to four and
altered the emphasis to include not only what was to become
a fourth lecture (added in this book as the chapter on Erich
Auerbach's humanist masterpiece *Mimesis*) but also a changed
political and social environment. These four lectures were
delivered at the generous invitation of the Centre for
Research in the Arts, Social Sciences, and Humanities
(CRASSH), headed by Professor Ian Donaldson at Cambridge University, where my wife Mariam and I enjoyed the

wonderful hospitality of King's College. I am most grateful to Ian and Grazia Donaldson for their warmth and marvelous spirit, and to Mary-Rose Cheadle, and Melanie Leggatt of CRASSH for their extraordinary solicitude and practical help. For Provost Pat Bateson and the Fellows of King's, we scarcely have words enough to express our gratitude for their hospitality during what was a trying time for me. It is ironic that both sets of lectures, in New York and in Cambridge, were given during intense periods of chemotherapy and transfusion, so I really needed and truly appreciated all the help I was given. The lectures have now been reworked and revised for publication.

What intervened between the two dates I mentioned above were the events of September 11, 2001. A changed political atmosphere has overtaken the United States and, to varying degrees, the rest of the world. The war against terrorism, the campaign in Afghanistan, the Anglo-American invasion of Iraq: all these have given rise to a world of heightened animosities, a much more aggressive American attitude towards the world, and—considering my own bicultural background—a much exacerbated conflict between what have been called "the West" and "Islam," labels I have long found both misleading and more suitable for the mobilization of collective passions than for lucid understanding unless they are deconstructed analytically and critically. Far more than they fight, cultures coexist and interact fruitfully with each other. It is to this idea of humanistic culture as coexistence and sharing that these pages are meant to contribute, and whether they succeed or not, I at least have the satisfaction of having tried.

Because of all these personal and general circumstances, my lectures on American humanism and its bearing on the world we live in are neither a definitive statement nor a call to arms. I shall of course let the pages that follow here speak for themselves, but I would like to say that I have tried in a reflective way to discuss those aspects of my enormous subject that have meant the most to me. For instance, I have always wondered how and in what ways humanism, normally thought of as a fairly restricted field of endeavor, relates to other dimensions of intellectual undertaking without becoming something like sociology or political science; this is what I discuss in the first chapter. In the second, having been a university student and teacher of the humanities for the past several decades, I thought it was important to take note of how the world of my education and the world I now live in are quite different, and how the duties of a humanist then are sometimes startlingly at odds with what is expected of us now—and never more so than after 9/11. In my third chapter, I discuss the crucial role of philology, which I use, alongside a description of attentive, imaginative close reading, in the hope that a trained openness to what a text says (and with that openness, a certain amount of resistance) is the royal road to humanistic understanding in the widest and best sense of the phrase.

I have further added a chapter that serves as a coda, entitled "The Public Role of Writers and Intellectuals," a piece written originally for an academic occasion, a conference on the republic of letters, held at Oxford University in September 2000. Substantial changes in this text also reflect the special atmosphere imposed on us by the terrible events of 9/11, but I'd like to note that the essential argument remains as I had originally written it.

EWS
New York, May 2003

HUMANISM AND
DEMOCRATIC CRITICISM

1

HUMANISM'S SPHERE

I SHOULD LIKE TO BEGIN THIS SET OF REFLECTIONS BY saying immediately that for all sorts of fairly compelling reasons, I shall be focusing on American humanism, although I do think that a good deal of my argument applies elsewhere too. I have lived in the United States for the majority of my adult life, and for the past four decades I have been a practicing humanist, a teacher, critic, and scholar. That is the world I know best. Second, as the world's only remaining superpower, America offers the humanist special challenges and demands, unlike those presented by any other nation. Clearly, though, as an immigrant society, the United States is not a homogenous place, and that, too, is part of the mix of factors that the American humanist is required to take into account. Thirdly, I grew up in a non-Western culture, and, as someone who is amphibious or bicultural, I am especially aware, I think, of perspectives and traditions other than those commonly thought of as uniquely American or "Western." This perhaps gives me a slightly peculiar angle. For example, the European antecedents of American humanism and those which derive from or are thought of as "outside" the Western purview interest me a great deal, and I shall be speaking about them in my third and fourth chapters and about how, in many ways, they derive from outside the Western tradition. Lastly, the setting in America and perhaps everywhere in the world has changed considerably since the terrible events of September 11, 2001, with dire consequences for us all. I take those into account, also, but here again, the American scene is special for quite obvious reasons.

The last thing I want to note at the outset is that the real subject of this book is not humanism *tout court*, which is a subject altogether too large and vague for what I am talking about here, but rather humanism and critical practice, humanism as it informs what one does as an intellectual and scholar-teacher of the humanities in today's turbulent world, which is now brimming over with belligerency, actual wars, and all kinds of terrorism. To say, with the young Georg Lukacs, that we live in a fragmented world abandoned by God, but not by his many noisy acolytes, is to risk understatement.

As I said above, I have been a teacher of literature and humanities at Columbia University since 1963. For various reasons, Columbia has offered a privileged place to view American humanism in the century that has just come to a close and the one just beginning. This is the university at which a celebrated, indeed legendary, set of required undergraduate core courses, typifying the liberal education, has been offered uninterruptedly for the past eighty-one years. At the heart of this curriculum is a year's sequence, established in 1937, entitled simply "The Humanities"; for several years now the sequence has been commonly known as the "Western Humanities" to distinguish it from a parallel offering called

"Eastern" or "Oriental" or "non-Western Humanities." The idea that every freshman or sophomore student must take this rigorous four-hour-per-week course has been absolutely, perhaps even indomitably, central in all sorts of positive ways to a Columbia College education, as much because of the almost terrifyingly major and central quality of the readings—Homer, Herodotus, Aeschylus, Euripides, Plato and Aristotle, the Bible, Virgil, Dante, Augustine, Shakespeare, Cervantes, and Dostoyevsky—as for the large amount of time lavished not only on those difficult authors and books but on defending the significance of reading them to the world at large. The Columbia humanities course emerged from the so-called culture wars of the 1970s and 1980s largely unscathed and unchanged.

I recall being asked, about twenty five years ago, to take part in a public panel discussion of the humanities sequence at the university, and I recall no less vividly that I was a minority of one when I criticized the course for having our students encounter Latin, Greek, Hebrew, Italian, French, and Spanish texts in sometimes undistinguished or nondescript translations. I made the point that the practice of reading these wonderful books out of their historical contexts and at several removes from their original forms needed some critical looking into and that misty-eyed pieties about what a great experience it is to read Dante—rather like the musings of aging former summer-campers about the good old days climbing Mount Washington, or some other such activity associated with pastoral habit and invented tradition—allied to the uncritical assumptions about "great books" disseminated by the course, which had somehow become an integral part of it, were open to justified suspicion. I did not at all suggest that the course be abandoned, but I did recommend that easy equations between "our" tradition, "the humanities," and "the greatest works" be abandoned. There are "other" traditions and, therefore, other humanities: surely those might somehow be taken into account and figured in as tempering the unexamined centrality of what was, in effect, a hammered-together confection of what comprised "ours." On the other hand, said my late colleague Lionel Trilling to me, the humanities course has the virtue of giving Columbia students a common basis in reading, and if they later forget the books (as many always do), at least they will have forgotten the same ones. This did not strike me as an overpowering argument, but, as opposed to not reading anything except technical literature in the social sciences and sciences, it was compelling nevertheless. I have since gone along with the gist of what the humanities course is best at doing, which is to acquaint students with the core literary and philosophical canon of Western cultures.

To mention Trilling here is to give considerable prominence to another of Columbia's claims so far as humanism is concerned. It is a university boasting, over a considerable length of time, a whole population of distinguished humanists, many of whom I have had the pleasure of working with or simply being here with. In addition to Trilling himself, there have been (to mention only the ones I knew or overlapped with as senior eminences when I came to New York in 1963) such figures as Mark van Doren, Jacques Barzun, F. W. Dupee, Andrew Chiappe, Moses Hadas, Gilbert Highet, Howard Porter, Paul Oskar Kristellar, Meyer Shapiro, Rufus Mathewson, Karl-Ludwig Selig, and Fritz Stern, among many others. Certainly it was true of most of these scholars that not only were they humanists in all traditional senses of the word, but they were also distinguished as notable examples of what academic humanism was and is at its best. Some of them—Trilling in particular—frequently spoke critically about liberal humanism, sometimes even disquietingly, although in the public eye and in the opinion of their aca-

demic colleagues and students, they represented the humanistic life, without jargon or undue professionalism, at its richest and most intense. Before these men—Columbia College
until only the last eighteen years being essentially a male
school—were such diverse figures as John Dewey, Randolph
Bourne, and Joel Springarn, whose work in philosophy, political thought, and literature had a major impact on defining
Columbia's commitment to the virtues of liberal and sometimes radical humanism as a component of the democratic
spirit and also to the continuing search for freedom, which
has been so well documented in America by my colleague
and friend Eric Foner in his excellent book *The Story of American Freedom.*

Much of this provides me with an auspicious background
for my inquiry into the relevance and future of humanism in
contemporary life, the subject to which these pages are dedicated. It also indicates how rich and how contested a field it
is, with all sorts of debates, polemics, and research projects
concerning the role and place of humanism and the humanities flooding the public realm during the closing years of the
past century and the beginning of this one. I have neither the
desire nor the capacity to recapitulate all those arguments nor
to undertake a long catalogue of the meanings of humanism,
except to note their encroaching presence on what I have to
say and to indicate that I shall be making highly selective use
of what others have said. My argument is intended as a con-
tinuation, within the Columbia context, of what my predecessors have said and done—predecessors, I hasten to add,
who have made my years at that institution so extraordinarily rich and valuable to me. Despite my involvement in the
struggle for Palestinian human rights, I have never taught
anything but the Western humanities at Columbia, literature
and music in particular, and I intend to go on doing so as long
as I can. But at the same time I think that the moment has

come, for me at least, to reconsider, reexamine, and reformu-
late the relevance of humanism as we head into a new mil-
lennium with so many circumstances undergoing enough
dramatic change to transform the setting entirely.

Therefore what follows in my first chapter is an extended
meditation on the useable scope of humanism as an ongoing
practice and not as a possession, on what humanistic activity
is about rather than a list of desirable attributes in a humanist, given a whole series of claims and counterclaims made on
behalf of humanism and the humanities by those who pro-
pose it as something they can speak for. In my second chapter, I shall try to give an account of what enormous changes
in the very basis for humanistic practice have already
occurred during the closing years of the twentieth century
and which need to be laid out very methodically in order to
understand what we can and cannot do now in the name and
under the aegis of humanism. In my third chapter, I shall suggest how philology, an undeservedly forgotten and musty-
sounding but intellectually compelling discipline, needs
somehow to be restored, reinvigorated, and made relevant to
the humanistic enterprise in today's United States. Last of all,
I shall speak about the greatest book of general humanistic
practice since World War II, Erich Auerbach's *Mimesis*, and
how it provides an enduring example for us today.

I should stress again that I am treating this subject not in
order to produce a history of humanism, nor an exploration
of all its possible meanings, and certainly not a thoroughgoing
examination of its metaphysical relationship to a prior Being
in the manner of Heidegger's "Letter on Humanism." What
concerns me is humanism as a useable praxis for intellectuals
and academics who want to know what they are doing, what
they are committed to as scholars, and who want also to connect these principles to the world in which they live as citizens. This necessarily involves a good deal of contemporary

history, some sociopolitical generalization, and above all a sharpened awareness of why humanism is important to this society at this time, more than ten years after the end of the Cold War, as the global economy is going through major transformations, and a new cultural landscape seems to be emerging, almost beyond the precedents of our experiences to date. The war on terrorism and the major military campaign in the Middle East, part of a new U.S. military doctrine of pre-emptive strikes, are not the least of the changed circumstances that the humanist must in some way confront. Besides, we are regularly prodded to reflect on the significance of humanism when so many of the words in current discourse have "human" (and implying "humane" and "humanistic") at their cores. NATO's bombing of Yugoslavia in 1999, for example, was described as a "humanitarian intervention," though many of its results struck people as deeply inhumane. A German intellectual is quoted as having called the whole NATO episode a new form of "military humanism." And why was it both "humanistic" and "humanitarian" to intervene there and not, say, in Rwanda or Turkey, where ethnic cleansing and mass killings have occurred on a wide scale? Similarly, according to Dennis Halliday, once the main UN official in charge of administering the oil-for-food program in Iraq, the results of the sanctions have been "inhumane and genocidal," an opinion which caused him to resign from his job in protest. Yet this, as well as the miserable fate of the Iraqi people (even as Saddam Hussein seems to have prospered during the sanctions), scarcely entered the discourse during the run-up to the proposed war, even when "liberating" the people of Iraq was one of the topics. And also, as scholars and teachers we believe we are right to call what we do "humanistic" and what we teach "the humanities." Are these still serviceable phrases, and if so in what way? How then may we view humanism as an activity in light of its past and of its probable future?

Since September 11, terror and terrorism have been thrust into the public consciousness with amazing insistence. In the United States, the principal emphasis has been on the distinction between our good and their evil. You are either with us, says George Bush, or against us. We represent a humane culture; they, violence and hatred. We are civilized; they are barbarians. Mixed in with all this are two flawed suppositions: one, that their civilization (Islam) is deeply opposed to ours (the West), a thesis vaguely based on Samuel Huntington's deplorably vulgar and reductive thesis of the clash of civilizations; second, the preposterous notion that to analyze the political history and even the nature of terror, in the process trying to define it, is equivalent to justifying it. I do not want to spend any time going over these notions or to try to refute them because, quite frankly, they strike me as trivial and superficial. I just want to note here their lingering presence and move on.

The most direct and concrete way for me to begin to get at humanism's scope is by way of a personal experience. One of the most searching and sympathetic early reviews of my book *Orientalism* was published in 1980, two years after the book's appearance, by James Clifford in the distinguished journal *History and Theory*. Clifford, who happened also to be the namesake and son of my older Columbia English Department colleague and friend, eighteenth-century scholar James Clifford, later included his essay-review as one of the chapters of his influential 1988 book *The Predicament of Culture*. One of the main and most often cited criticisms he made was that there was a serious inconsistency lodged at my book's heart, the conflict between my avowed and unmistakable humanistic bias and the antihumanism of my subject and my approach toward it. Clifford laments "the relapse into the essentializing modes it [*Orientalism*] attacks," and he complains that the book "is ambivalently enmeshed in the totalizing habits of

Western humanism" (Clifford, 271). A little later in his essay (and it's precisely this sort of observation that made Clifford so useful a critic) he goes on to say that my "complex critical posture," inconsistencies and all, cannot be dismissed as merely aberrant but is in fact symptomatic of the book's "unrestful predicament . . . its methodological ambivalences [which, he added] are characteristic of an increasingly global experience" (275). The interesting point here is the way Clifford characterizes humanism as something fundamentally discordant with advanced theory of the kind I particularly stressed and drew on, Michel Foucault's, a theory that Clifford correctly sees as having largely disposed of humanism's essentializing and totalizing modes.

And in many ways Clifford was right, since during the 1960s and 1970s the advent of French theory in the humanistic departments of American and English universities had brought about a severe if not crippling defeat of what was considered traditional humanism by the forces of structuralism and post-structuralism, both of which professed the death of man-the-author and asserted the preeminence of antihumanist systems such as those found in the work of Lévi-Strauss, Foucault himself, and Roland Barthes. The sovereignty of the subject—to use the technical phrase for what Enlightenment thought did with Descartes's notion of the *cogito*, which was to make it the center of all human knowledge and hence capable of essentializing thought in itself— was challenged by what Foucault and Lévi-Strauss carried forward from the work of thinkers such as Marx, Freud, Nietzsche, and the linguist Ferdinand de Saussure. This group of pioneers showed, in effect, that the existence of systems of thinking and perceiving transcended the powers of individual subjects, individual humans who were inside those systems (systems such as Freud's "unconscious" or Marx's "capital") and therefore had no power over them, only the choice either to use or be used by them. This of course flatly contradicts the core of humanistic thought, and hence the individual *cogito* was displaced, or demoted, to the status of illusory autonomy or fiction.

Although I was one of the first critics to engage with and discuss French theory in the American university, Clifford correctly saw that I somehow remained unaffected by that theory's ideological antihumanism, mainly, I think, because I did not (and still do not) see in humanism only the kind of totalizing and essentializing trends that Clifford identified. Nor have I been convinced of the arguments put forward in the wake of structuralist antihumanism by postmodernism or by its dismissive attitudes to what Jean-Francois Lyotard famously called the grand narratives of enlightenment and emancipation. On the contrary, as a fair degree of my own political and social activism has assured me, people all over the world can be and are moved by ideals of justice and equality—the South African victory in the liberation struggle is a perfect case in point—and the affiliated notion that humanistic ideals of liberty and learning still supply most disadvantaged people with the energy to resist unjust war and military occupation, for instance, and to try to overturn despotism and tyranny, both strike me as ideas that are alive and well. And despite the (in my opinion) shallow but influential ideas of a certain facile type of radical antifoundationalism, with its insistence that real events are at most linguistic effects, and its close relative, the end-of-history thesis, these are so contradicted by the historical impact of human agency and labor as to make a detailed refutation of them here unnecessary. Change is human history, and human history as made by human action and understood accordingly is the very ground of the humanities.

I believed then, and still believe, that it is possible to be critical of humanism in the name of humanism and that,

schooled in its abuses by the experience of Eurocentrism and
empire, one could fashion a different kind of humanism that
was cosmopolitan and text-and-language-bound in ways that
absorbed the great lessons of the past from, say, Erich Auerbach and Leo Spitzer and more recently from Richard
Poirier, and still remain attuned to the emergent voices and
currents of the present, many of them exilic, extraterritorial,
and unhoused, as well as uniquely American. For my purposes
here, the core of humanism is the secular notion that the historical world is made by men and women, and not by God,
and that it can be understood rationally according to the
principle formulated by Vico in *New Science*, that we can
really know only what we make or, to put it differently, we
can know things according to the way they were made. His
formula is known as the verum/factum equation, which is to
say that as human beings in history we know what we make,
or rather, to know is to know how a thing is made, to see it
from the point of view of its human maker. Hence Vico's
notion also of *sapienza poetica*, historical knowledge based on
the human being's capacity to make knowledge, as opposed
to absorbing it passively, reactively, and dully.

There is one provision in Vico's theory that I'd like particularly to emphasize. Early in *New Science*, he lists an exhaustive
set of "elements," or principles, out of which he says his
method will be derived as the book progresses. Moreover, he
adds, "and just as the blood does animate inanimate bodies, so
will these elements course through our Science and animate it
in all its reasonings about the common nature of nations"
(Vico, 60). A moment later, he seems to undermine the whole
prospect of knowledge by observing as a cardinal principle
that "because of the indefinite nature of the human mind,
wherever it is lost in ignorance man makes himself the measure of things." Now there is no doubt that Vico also believes
that humanistic knowledge does exist and that it arises from

primitive, or what he calls poetic, thought and over time develops into philosophic knowledge. Despite the progress, despite the certainty and truth of later knowledge, Vico, I believe, takes the tragic view that human knowledge is permanently undermined by the "indefinite nature of the human mind." (This is quite different from John Gray's notion in *Straw Dogs: Thoughts on Humans and Other Animals*, that science disposes of humanism, which he says is equivalent only to a belief in human progress: this rather constricted equation, I think, is far from central, if indeed it occurs at all, in thinking about humanism.) One can acquire philosophy and knowledge, it is true, but the basically unsatisfactory fallibility (rather than its constant improvement) of the human mind persists nonetheless. So there is always something radically incomplete, insufficient, provisional, disputable, and arguable about humanistic knowledge that Vico never loses sight of and that, as I said, gives the whole idea of humanism a tragic flaw that is constitutive to it and cannot be removed. This flaw can be remedied and mitigated by the disciplines of philological learning and philosophic understanding, as we shall see in my next two chapters, but it can never be superceded. Another way of putting this is to say that the subjective element in humanistic knowledge and practice has to be recognized and in some way reckoned with since there is no use in trying to make a neutral, mathematical science out of it. One of the main reasons that Vico wrote his book was to contest the Cartesian thesis that there could be clear and distinct ideas and that those were free not only of the actual mind that has them, but of history as well. That kind of idea, Vico contends, is simply impossible where history and the individual humanist are concerned. And while it is certainly the case that history is more than its encumbrances, those play a crucial role nonetheless.

It must be remembered that antihumanism took hold on the United States intellectual scene partly because of widespread revulsion with the Vietnam War. Part of that revulsion was the emergence of a resistance movement to racism, imperialism generally, and the dry-as-dust academic humanities that had for years represented an unpolitical, unworldly, and oblivious (sometimes even manipulative) attitude to the present, all the while adamantly extolling the virtues of the past, the untouchability of the canon, and the superiority of "how we used to do it"—superiority, that is, to the disquieting appearance on the intellectual and academic scene of such things as women's, ethnic, gay, cultural, and postcolonial studies and, above all I believe, a loss of interest in and the vitiation of the core idea of the humanities. The centrality of the great literary texts was now threatened not only by popular culture but by the heterogeneity of upstart or insurgent philosophy, politics, linguistics, psychoanalysis, and anthropology. All these factors may have done a great deal to discredit the ideology, if not the committed practice, of humanism.

But it is worth insisting, in this as well as other cases, that attacking the abuses of something is not the same thing as dismissing or entirely destroying that thing. So, in my opinion, it has been the abuse of humanism that discredits some of humanism's practitioners without discrediting humanism itself. Yet in the past four or five years, an enormous outpouring of books and articles has, in a vast overreaction to this purported or attempted antihumanism—which in most cases was an often idealistic critique of humanism's misuses in politics and public policy, many of which were in regard to non-European people and immigrants—gone on to diagnose such lugubrious improbabilities as the death of literature or the failure of humanism to respond robustly enough to the new challenges. Nor have these vehement jeremiads about the practice of literary study come only from irate traditionalists or callow polemicists like Lynn Cheney, Dinesh D'Souza, and Roger Kimball. They have also come somewhat more understandably from young people, graduate students especially, who have been bitterly disappointed that there are no jobs for them or that they have to teach many hours of remedial courses in several institutions as adjuncts or part-timers without health benefits, tenure, or prospects for advancement. In some cases, venerable institutions like the Modern Language Association have come to seem like the cause of our current predicament, and the university itself, as utopian a place as exists in this society, has also come under attack.

That the humanities as a whole have lost their eminence in the university is, nonetheless, undoubtedly true. As Masao Miyoshi has claimed in a series of densely argued essays, the late-twentieth-century American university has been corporatized and to a certain degree annexed by defense, medical, biotechnical, and corporate interests, who are much more concerned with funding projects in the natural sciences than they are in the humanities. Miyoshi goes on to say that the humanities—which, he correctly supposes, is not the province of the corporate manager but of the humanist—have fallen into irrelevance and quasi-medieval fussiness, ironically enough because of the fashionability of newly relevant fields like postcolonialism, ethnic studies, cultural studies, and the like. This has effectively detoured the humanities from its rightful concern with the critical investigation of values, history, and freedom, turning it, it would seem, into a whole factory of word-spinning and insouciant specialties, many of them identity-based, that in their jargon and special pleading address only like-minded people, acolytes, and other academics. If we don't respect ourselves, he says, why should anyone else, and so we wither away, unmourned and unnoticed. The humanities have become harmless as well as powerless to affect anyone or anything. Even Miyoshi, I hasten to add, is not dismissing the humanities or humanism out of hand. Quite the contrary.

It should already be clear that in speaking about humanism so far, a number of implications and assumptions have
been operating, as they routinely do in examinations that take
it for granted that humanism has much to do with education
generally and university curricula in particular. What comes
to mind straight away is the distinction made between a collective group of subjects called the humanities, on the one
hand, and two other collective groups, the social and natural
sciences on the other. C. P. Snow's forty-year-old thesis about
the two separated cultures seems to hold up more or less,
despite considerable overlap between them in recent debates
over biomedical ethics, environmental issues, and human and
civil rights, to mention only a few complex, interdisciplinary
fields of inquiry.

Looking back over the uses of the word "humanism" for
the past century or so, one can see that further themes and
problematics stand out, almost as steadily as the opposition
with the social and natural sciences. One, which I have
adopted as a simple working definition for my argument
here, is that the humanities concern secular history, the products of human labor, the human capacity for articulate
expression. Borrowing a phrase from R. S. Crane, we can say
that the humanities "consist in all those things which . . . are
therefore not amenable to adequate explanation in terms of
general laws of natural processes, physical or biological, or in
terms [only] of collective social conditions or forces. . . . They
are, in short, what we commonly speak of as human achievements" (Crane, 1:8). Humanism is the achievement of form
by human will and agency; it is neither system nor impersonal
force like the market or the unconscious, however much one
may believe in the workings of both.

Having said that, I can see a small handful of crucial problems located at the very heart of what humanism today is or
might be, allowing for the time being that both humanism

and literature, understood as the dedicated study of good and important writing, have an especially close relationship with each other that I want to highlight in these reflections.

The first problem is a frequent but not always admitted connection between humanism as an attitude or practice that is often associated with very selective elites, be they religious, aristocratic, or educational, on the one hand, and, on the other, with an attitude of stern opposition, sometimes stated, sometimes not, to the idea that humanism might or could be a democratic process producing a critical and progressively freer mind. In other words, humanism is thought of as something very restricted and difficult, like a rather austere club with rules that keep most people out and, when some are allowed in, a set of regulations disallowing anything that might expand the club's membership, make it less restricted a place, or make it more pleasurable a location to be in. The theory that dominated humanities departments until it provoked the attacks and dismissals of the antihumanist revolution of the 1960s and 1970s was strongly influenced by T. S. Eliot and, later, by the Southern Agrarians and New Critics: namely, that humanism was a special attainment that required the cultivating or reading of certain difficult texts and, in the process, the giving up of certain things, like amusement, pleasure, relevance to worldly circumstances, and so on. It was Dante, not Shakespeare who was the presiding figure here, along with a belief that only compressed, difficult, and rare forms of art, forms inaccessible to anyone who did not have the requisite training, were worth bothering with. Who can forget Eliot's narrow quibbles about Shakespeare, Johnson, Dickens, and numerous others whom he did not consider serious or grave or hieratic enough? Or, in the nearly contemporaneous work of F. R. Leavis, there was an equally stern, unsmiling affirmation of the few, the very few works that could be considered truly great.

In various books on the crisis in literary humanism that occurred after midcentury, Richard Ohmann and several others have interestingly discussed the ascendancy and gradual eclipse of this orthodoxy, indicating how deliberately the humanities were imagined and taught as not having much to do with the sordid world of contemporary history, politics, and economics. These, according to Eliot, in his famous lectures at the University of Virginia 1934, compiled in *After Strange Gods*, furnished us with a panorama of waste and futility. Aside from segregating the world of literature and art behind a whole series of walls, this orthodoxy stressed literature's formality (perhaps unduly under the influence of a misreading of high modernism) and the supposed spiritual and redemptive improvements offered by extremely rarified kinds of writing. It was the almost sacrosanct, pastoral past that literature and humanism hallowed, and neither the process of making history nor of changing it. Ohmann demonstrates that when they are turned into a kind of professional code, these attitudes congeal all too easily into a routine complacency, which claims that a dispassionate search for truth, detachment, and disengagement constitutes the proper pursuit of literary study.

It was not a big step from the world of High Anglican humanism presided over by Eliot to the reemergence of what might charitably be called reductive and didactic humanism in the work, and person, of a very narrow kind of educational conservative typified by Allan Bloom, whose *Closing of the American Mind* caused such a stir when it first appeared (with a foreword by Saul Bellow) and became a best-seller in 1987. I call this a reemergence because sixty years before Bloom, a school of what were called New Humanists, whose principal members were Irving Babbit and Paul Elmer More, had already berated American education, culture, and academics for abandoning the classical worldview typified (tautologi-

cally enough) by the classics, Sanskrit, and a few literary monuments or languages which they happened to teach as an
antidote for what Bellow, in his preface to Bloom's book, calls
"Health, Sex, Race, War." All these, he argued like the New
Humanists before him, had turned the university into "a con-
ceptual warehouse of often harmful influences" (Bellow, 18).
(See, in this connection, the more sophisticated arguments
about works that should not be read or taught in *Forbidden
Knowledge*, by Roger Shattuck, a critic whose work I generally admire.)

What Bloom and his predecessors shared, in addition to a
common dyspepsia of tone, was a feeling that the doors of
humanism had been left open to every sort of unruly indi-
vidualism, disreputable modishness, and uncanonized learning, with the result that true humanism had been violated, if
not altogether discredited. This was another way of saying that
too many undesirable non-Europeans had suddenly appeared
at "our" gates. Bellow's enlightened and liberal embodiment
of what he and Bloom (and Babbit before them) really dis-
liked about the new spirit is dispiritingly evident when, in *Mr.
Sammler's Planet,* the Nobel prize–winning author has a
nameless African American bus passenger pull down his
trousers and display his pudenda to the saintly, and humanistic, Mr. Sammler.

For Allan Bloom, whose book seems to me to represent
the nadir of what Richard Hofstader calls anti–intellectualism
in American life, education ideally was to be a matter less of
investigation, criticism, and humanistic enlargement of consciousness than a series of unsmiling restrictions, ending up
with a small handful of elites, a smaller reading list of a few
Greek and French Enlightenment authors, and a very long list
of enemies, including the relatively harmless Brigitte Bardot
and Yoko Ono. There's little original in Bloom's book, alas,
since what he successfully taps into is an unpleasant Ameri-

can penchant (lamented a long time ago by Henry James) for moralizing reductiveness, mostly in the form of formulas of what not to do and read, what to consider as culture and what not. There is a marvelous observation on this score in an essay about Matthew Arnold by Henry James, where James says about America that "the curiosity with regard to culture is extreme in that country; if there is in some quarters a considerable uncertainty as to what it may consist of, there is everywhere a great wish to get hold of it, at least on trial" (James, 730). Far from considering that universities were the solution to the problem of culture's nature, Bloom, like his predecessors Babbitt, More, and Norman Foerster, found that universities were themselves the problem, catering to the age's permissive materialism, its far too popular trends, and its volatile unethical tendencies. But where, except in the university, could Babbitt and his followers have been tolerated for their intolerance, their monotony of tone, and the unremitting complaint of their message?

It's difficult not to read the New Humanists of the 1920s and 1930s with Allan Bloom in mind and not see in all of them what the historian Jackson Lears has called American antimodernism. In their cult of an almost sacralized past (when things were "better ordered") and their prescriptions for a small elite not only of readers but of writers, all these defenders of humanism equate the decline of standards primly, and in some way even despairingly, with modernity itself. They follow in the general path opened by Ortega y Gasset in his famous pamphlet *The Dehumanization of Art*, by eccentrically conservative English intellectuals such as H. G. Wells, Kipling, the Bloomsbury group, and D. H. Lawrence, and by the greatest romantic antimodernist of them all, the early Georg Lukacs. In all these cases, a key pillar of faith is a surreptitious equation between popular and multicultural, multilingual democracy, on the one hand, and a horrendous decline in humanistic and aesthetic, not to say also ethical, standards, on the other. Hence the common recourse for redemption to a privileged, suitably laundered elite that, with typical antinomian perversity in the American case, is to be found in precisely those same depraved universities where, if Bloom and his followers were to have their way, a carefully engineered curriculum and a scrubbed-clean and tiny student body would set right most of the problems. Only by proper education could a new elite come into being, and this elite, given the style and undoubted popular audience solicited by the ultra-astringent Bloom, is, peculiarly enough, supposed to have a mass appeal. Soon even Bloom's relatively sophisticated rhetoric was overtaken by William Bennett's thumping oratory about reclaiming a heritage and a core of traditional values, which also attained great popular acclaim. These have once again been trundled out in the aftermath of 9/11, as a way of justifying America's apparently limitless war against evil. How odd it is that these two vehement attacks on the popular spirit, so to speak, addressed their complaints to large numbers of ordinary Americans who by definition could not, except by self-denial and self-mutilation, ever attain the favored status advocated by Bloom and Bennett for a tiny privileged elite. America's is an immigrant society composed now less of Northern Europeans than of Latinos, Africans, and Asians; why should this fact not be reflected in "our" traditional values and heritage?

Jackson Lears quite fascinatingly draws connections between, on the one hand, the American variety of antimodernism that spawned the New Humanists and their later followers and, on the other, a whole host of quite special currents in American society such as the cults of war and spiritual ecstasy, conspicuous consumption, and the quest for feel-good self-fulfillment. These are complex matters that I cannot get into here except to note that to the outsider's eye, all this antimodern sentiment is most economically symbolized by an unfortunate frown, a stern facade of disapproval, and a hectoring asceticism that dismisses the pleasures and discoveries of humanism out of hand. I refer to the spirit of the original humanism that we correctly associate in the Atlantic West with Erasmus's Folly, Rabelais's Abbe Thélème, and Cola di Rienzi's *virtú*. Nothing in any of these, or in Aretino, Montaigne, Ficino, and Thomas More has much to do with the sour pursing of the lips that expresses the joylessness and disapproval of the New Humanists and their later followers. Instead, there arises out of the dour exertions of New Humanism a surprisingly narrow-minded chauvinism that amazingly scants the fact that America is after all an absolutely heterogeneous society, ideologically committed to the broadest possible republicanism and opposed to hereditary, as well as manufactured, elites and aristocracies.

Read through most of the lamentations of today that decry the absence of standards, that long for the days of Perry Miller and Douglas Bush, that keep talking about literature sequestered from the world of human history and labor, that decry the presence of women's and gender studies, of African and Asian literatures, that pretend that the humanities and humanism are the prerogative only of a select handful of English-educated people uninfected by illusions about progress, freedom, and modernity, and you will be hard put to explain how such a refrain is sounded in a radically multicultural society such as America's. Is it necessarily the case that a belief in humanism as an educational and cultural ideal must be accompanied by reams of laundry-list exclusions, the prevalence of a miniscule class of selected and approved authors and readers, and a tone of mean-spirited rejection? I would say no, since to understand humanism at all, for us as citizens of this particular republic, is to understand it as democratic, open to all classes and backgrounds, and as a process

of unending disclosure, discovery, self-criticism, and liberation. I would go so far as to say that humanism is critique, critique that is directed at the state of affairs in, as well as out of,
the university (which is certainly not the position adopted by
the carping and narrow humanism that sees itself as an elite
formation) and that gathers its force and relevance by its
democratic, secular, and open character.

For there is, in fact, no contradiction at all between the
practice of humanism and the practice of participatory citizenship. Humanism is not about withdrawal and exclusion.
Quite the reverse: its purpose is to make more things available
to critical scrutiny as the product of human labor, human
energies for emancipation and enlightenment, and, just as
importantly, human misreadings and misinterpretations of the
collective past and present. There was never a misinterpreta-
tion that could not be revised, improved, or overturned. There
was never a history that could not to some degree be recovered and compassionately understood in all its suffering and
accomplishment. Conversely, there was never a shameful
secret injustice or a cruel collective punishment or a mani-
festly imperial plan for domination that could not be exposed,
explained, and criticized. Surely, that too is at the heart of
humanistic education, despite all the supposedly neoconserv-
ative philosophy condemning whole classes and races to eternal backwardness, proving—if that's the right word—in the
worst Darwinian sense that some people deserve ignorance,
poverty, ill health, and backwardness according to the free
market, while others can somehow be fashioned by think-
tank projects and policies into the new elites.

If this first problem, or rather syndrome, that I have been
describing begins and ends in a social rejection of what is
modern and an espousal of a supposedly older, supposedly
more humanistic and authentic ideal of association—embodied in the small elite or cabalistic quasi aristocracy—the next

issue or problem within the discourse of humanism that I
want to discuss is of an epistemological cast. It derives from a
supposed opposition between what is designated as traditional
and canonical and the unwelcome interventions of the new
and the intellectually representative of the age we live in.
Unfortunately, many of the same impoverishing hobbles that
we already found reappear here as well. Of course, we need to
defend language against jargon and unintelligibility, but those
need not be understood as symptoms of how depraved and
objectionable is everything new. All language exists to be revi-
talized by change. Look at the whole history of humanism
and criticism—the two are invariably associated—in as many
cultures and periods as you can assess, and you will find that
no great humanistic achievement was ever without an important component, relationship, or acceptance of the new, of
what is most newly true and exciting in the art, thought, or
culture of that period. This was true, for instance, of Euripides, whose last and greatest play, *The Bacchae*, was exactly
about resisting the new—and not surviving the effort. It was
even true of the greatest of all traditional masters, Johann
Sebastian Bach, whose work was a *summum* of canonical German polyphonic art as well as an opening to the influences of
the latest French and Italian dance styles.

There is no end of examples to this general rule, which
completely blows away the reactionary thesis that a veneration of the traditional or canonical must be opposed to the
innovations of contemporary art and thought. This is a very
far cry from Walter Benjamin's more severe—and true—
observation that every document of civilization is also a document of barbarism, a notion that seems to me essentially a
tragic humanistic truth of great significance, completely lost
on the new humanists for whom the approved culture is salu-
brious in an unadulterated, and finally uncomplicatedly
redemptive way. But since America, to all the people who

came here, represented the new in promise and hope, there seems every good reason to tie American humanism very resolutely to the energies, the jolts, the surprises and swerves of what is always present and arriving here in some form as the new and different.

Because the world has become far more integrated and demographically mixed than ever before, the whole concept of national identity has to be revised and, in most places that I know, is in the process of being revised. Muslims from North Africa, Kurds, Turks, and Arabs from the Middle East, West and East Indians, as well as men and women from several African countries have changed forever the collective face of Britain, Sweden, France, Germany, Italy, and Spain, among other countries in Europe. Extraordinary mixtures of nationalities, races, and religions form the different histories of Latin America, and when we look at India, Malaysia, Sri Lanka, Singapore, and several more Asian countries, we will note, as we would in the case of many African countries, an enormous variety of languages and cultures, most of them coexisting and interacting peacefully with each other in the normal course of events. The point is that of all the baggage inherited from nineteenth-century political thought, it is the notion of a unified, coherent, homogenous national identity that is now undergoing the most rethinking, and this change is being felt in every sphere of society and politics. The French and German stand against the U.S. war in Iraq, for instance, derives in large measure from the presence in those countries of sizeable Muslim or Arab minorities. School curricula, dress, media programs, and public discourse are all affected by the new mixtures that have emerged in the past two or three decades. In South Africa alone, there are now eleven official languages, which educational institutions must somehow take into account. The actual composition of America is not much different in diversity and multiplicity of cultures, although one unfortunate consequence has been the felt need to try to homogenize all this into an assertive, not to say bellicose and positive American identitarian unanimity. The invention of tradition has become far too thriving a business.

Some etymologists speculate that the word "canon" (as in "canonical") is related to the Arabic word "*qanun*," or law in the binding, legalistic sense of that word. But that is only one rather restrictive meaning. The other is a musical one, canon as a contrapuntal form employing numerous voices in usually strict imitation of each other, a form, in other words, expressing motion, playfulness, discovery, and, in the rhetorical sense, invention. Viewed this way, the canonical humanities, far from being a rigid tablet of fixed rules and monuments bullying us from the past—like Wagner's Beckmesser marking the youthful Walther's mistakes in *Die Meistersinger*—will always remain open to changing combinations of sense and signification; every reading and interpretation of a canonical work reanimates it in the present, furnishes an occasion for rereading, allows the modern and the new to be situated together in a broad historical field whose usefulness is that it shows us history as an agonistic process still being made, rather than finished and settled once and for all.

Much as I have admired and studied Jonathan Swift over the years, it used to be a source of regret for me that his attitudes about the past, as exemplified in his sympathies for ancients over moderns in the *Battle of the Books*, were so doctrinaire and unyielding. Until, that is, it became possible following the example of Yeats to read Swift in a revisionist way, as a demonic and tigerish a writer as has ever lived. Yeats magnanimously envisioned Swift's internal world essentially in a ceaseless conflict with itself, unsatisfied, unappeased, unreconciled in an almost Adornian way, rather than as settled into untroubled patterns of tranquility and unchanging order. So it is with the canon, which one can either venerate from afar or more actively wrestle with, using aspects of modernity in the struggle to evade a lifeless monumentality of the kind that Nietzsche and Emerson so properly decried.

Lastly, the third problem: so far as the historical presence of the humanities is concerned, two views are locked in interminable combat. One view interprets the past as an essentially complete history; the other sees history, even the past itself, as still unresolved, still being made, still open to the presence and the challenges of the emergent, the insurgent, the unrequited, and the unexplored. Maybe there is, as some have argued, a Western canon that is marmoreally finished in itself, before which we need to bow down. Maybe there is such a past; maybe we should venerate it. People seem to like that sort of thing. I don't. It doesn't strike me as sufficiently interesting or appropriate or imaginative. Besides, every culture, everywhere, as I said above, is now going through a massive process of self-definition, self-examination, and self-analysis, both with regard to the present and the past: in Asia, Africa, Europe, Latin America. It is ridiculous for pompous American academics to say that this is all too much turbulence—and therefore we want to go back to the Graeco-Roman past. Not to see that the essence of humanism is to understand human history as a continuous process of self-understanding and self-realization, not just for us, as white, male, European, and American, but for everyone, is to see nothing at all. There are other learned traditions in the world, there are other cultures, there are other geniuses. A superb sentence by Leo Spitzer, as brilliant a reader of texts as this century has produced and who spent his last years as an American humanist of European origin and training, is singularly apt. "The Humanist," he says, "believes in the power of the human mind of investigating the human mind" (Spitzer, 24). Note that Spitzer does not say the European mind, or only the Western canon. He talks about the human mind *tout court*.

This catholicity of vision is not at all what we have been getting from Harold Bloom, who has become the popular spokesman of the most extreme kind of dismissive aestheticism calling itself canonical humanism. His startling gifts have not prevented him from making the crudest and most blind attacks on what, in a shocking misreading of Wildean aestheticism, he supposes himself to be representing. Wilde was rather the most generous and radical of Irish readers, not at all the self-satisfied, stupefied, pseudo–Anglo aristocrat that poorly informed readers have made him out to be. In his incessant, grab-bag evocations of what he dismissively calls the school of resentment, Bloom includes everything said or written by the non-European, non-male, non-Anglo educated upstarts who don't happen to agree with his tiresome vatic trumpetings. Certainly one can accept, as I do, the existence of greater as well as lesser achievements in the arts, and even achievements that are entirely uninteresting (no one can like everything, after all): but I would never admit that something was humanistically, intrinsically uninteresting just because it was not one of ours or because it belonged to a different tradition or came from a different perspective and experience and was the result of different processes of work, as in Saul Bellow's appallingly condescending phrase, "show me the Zulu Proust."

Bloom's opinions about the humanistic canon show an absence rather than an invigorating presence of mind: he nearly always refuses to answer questions at public lectures, he refuses to engage with other arguments, he simply asseverates, affirms, intones. This is self-puffery, not humanism, and certainly not enlightened criticism. One should have as little truck with this sort of superficiality as with Samuel Huntington's clash of civilizations thesis: both result in the same bellicose dismissiveness; both radically misapprehend what it is about cultures and civilizations that makes them interesting—

not their essence or purity, but their combinations and diversity, their countercurrents, the way that they have had of conducting a compelling dialogue with other civilizations. And both Bloom and Huntington completely miss what has long been a characteristic of all cultures, namely, that there is a strong streak of radical antiauthoritarian dissent in them. It is ironic how such belligerent authoritarians as Bloom and Huntington have forgotten that many of the figures in today's canon were yesterday's insurgents.

For reasons I shall examine in my next chapter, there can be no true humanism whose scope is limited to extolling patriotically the virtues of our culture, our language, our monuments. Humanism is the exertion of one's faculties in language in order to understand, reinterpret, and grapple with the products of language in history, other languages and other histories. In my understanding of its relevance today, humanism is not a way of consolidating and affirming what "we" have always known and felt, but rather a means of questioning, upsetting, and reformulating so much of what is presented to us as commodified, packaged, uncontroversial, and uncritically codified certainties, including those contained in the masterpieces herded under the rubric of "the classics." Our intellectual and cultural world is now scarcely a simple, self-evident collection of expert discourses: it is rather a seething discordance of unresolved notations, to use Raymond Williams's fine word for the endlessly ramifying and elaborated articulations of culture.

Yet language is where we start from as humanists. One of the best ways of putting this in the specifically American context that is my concern here is to use a passage by Richard Poirier in his book *The Renewal of Literature*. In a chapter about Emerson entitled "The Question of Genius," Poirier states that for Emerson, "the most potent and unavoidable instrument of inherited culture was language itself," and language, as I have been saying in this lecture, supplies humanism with its basic material as well as, in literature, its richest occasion. But while supple and flexible, language provides us with "our social and cultural fate," which is why, Poirier points out, "we must first see it for what it is, and its form, ultimately, is the language we use in learning," and, I would add, in humanism, to know ourselves. But, Poirier sagely continues, "language is also the place wherein we can most effectively register our dissent from our fate by means of our troping, punning, parodistic echoings, and by letting vernacular energies play against revered terminologies. . . . Language is the only way to get around the obstruction of language" (72). In what follows I shall try to elucidate the changing situation both of language and of humanistic practice at the present time.

References

Bellow, Saul. "Health, Sex, Race, War." Foreword to *The Closing of the American Mind*, by Allan Bloom. New York: Simon and Schuster, 1987.

——. *Mr. Sammler's Planet*. New York, Viking Press, 1970.

Clifford, James. Review of *Orientalism*. *History and Theory* 19, no. 2 (February 1980): 204–23. Reprint, "On Orientalism." In *The Predicament of Culture: Twentieth-Century Ethnography, Literature, and Art*, by James Clifford, 255–76. Cambridge, Mass.: Harvard University Press, 1988.

Crane, R. S. *The Idea of the Humanities and Other Essays Critical and Historical*. 2 vols. Chicago: University of Chicago Press, 1968.

Eliot, T. S. *After Strange Gods: A Primer of Modern Heresy*. London: Faber and Faber, Limited, 1934.

Foner, Eric. *The Story of American Freedom*. New York: W. W. Norton & Company, 1999.

Gray, John. *Straw Dogs: Thoughts on Human and Other Animals*. London: Granta, 2002.

Heidegger, Martin. "Letter on Humanism." In *Martin Heidegger: Pathmarks*, ed. W. McNeill, Cambridge: Cambridge University Press, 1998.

Hofstader, Richard. *Anti-Intellectualism in American Life*. New York:
    Random House, 1966.

James, Henry. "Matthew Arnold." In *Literary Criticism: Essays on
    Literature, American Writers, English Writers*, ed. Leon Edel and
    Mark Wilson, 719–731. New York: Library of America, 1984.

Lears, T. J. Jackson. *No Place of Grace: Antimodernism and the Transfor-
    mation of American Culture, 1880–1920*. Chicago: University of
    Chicago Press, 1981.

Miyoshi, Masao. " 'Globalization,' Culture, and the University." In
    Cultures of Globalization, ed. Masao Miyoshi and Fredric
    Jameson, 247–70. Durham: Duke University Press, 1998.

——. "Ivory Tower in Escrow." *boundary 2* 27, no. 1 (Spring 2000):
    8–50.

——. "The University and the 'Global' Economy: The Cases of
    the United States and Japan." *South Atlantic Quarterly* 99, no. 4
    (2000): 669–96.

Ohmann, Richard. *English in America: A Radical View of the Profes-
    sion*. Oxford: Oxford University Press, 1976.

Ortega y Gassett, José. *Velasquez, Goya, and the Dehumanization of
    Art*. New York: W. W. Norton & Company, 1972.

Poirier, Richard. *The Renewal of Literature: Emersonian Reflections*.
    New York: Random House, 1987.

Shattuck, Roger. *Forbidden Knowledge: From Prometheus to Pornogra-
    phy*. New York: St. Martin's Press, 1996.

Snow, C. P. *The Two Cultures*. Cambridge: Cambridge University
    Press, 1959.

Spitzer, Leo. *Linguistics and Literary History: Essays in Stylistics*.
    Princeton, N.J.: Princeton Univesisty Press, 1948.

Vico, Giambattista. *The New Science of Giambattista Vico: Revised
    Translations of the Third Edition of 1744*. Trans. Thomas G.
    Bergin and Max H. Fisch. Ithaca: Cornell Univeristy Press,
    1984.

2

THE CHANGING BASES OF HUMANISTIC STUDY AND PRACTICE

IN THE PROCESS OF READING AND PREPARING FOR THIS BOOK, I found myself inevitably drawn to various collections of papers, symposia, reports, and the like concerning the state of the humanities both here and abroad. They reminded me of the so-called condition of England pamphlets and studies that seemed to proliferate ceaselessly in late-Victorian England. Perhaps the most remarkable result of my course of study has been the discovery that no matter who is writing or speaking, where, when, or to whom, the humanities always seem to be in deep and usually terminal trouble. The word "crisis" is the inevitable one here, whether it is for a group of distinguished academics, including Cleanth Brooks, Nathan Pusey, and Howard Mumford Jones at the University of Wisconsin in 1950, or another, later group, comprising Jonathan Culler, George Levine, and Catharine Stimpson, assembled at SUNY–Stony Brook by that university and the American Council of Learned Societies in May 1988.

Separated by almost forty years, yet using very similar terms, both sets of genuinely concerned American scholar-critics bewail the times in general, the increasing inroads on the humanities made by technology, specialization, and an inclement (in the later case, a decidedly hostile) popular climate. And once the exercise of self-blame is over, both repeat ringing phrases of endorsement that stress the importance of the humanities, phrases with which it is impossible to disagree, since both assemblies also argue that there is a core of humanity (stipulated in very eloquent language) that should not be violated by humanists but rather enhanced and variously emphasized. This is a bit like Alice boxing her own ears for cheating herself at croquet!

What has not changed from one period to another is the unstated feeling that colloquies of this kind, whose perennial goal is to gather well-known figures who will issue credible assertions in favor of their fields, are the public and momentarily influential culminations of many hours of classroom teaching and lecturing, library research and scholarly exchange (most of them obviously hidden from general view), all to ensure that the practice of teaching and criticism can continue for another period of time, waiting for the next such gathering to take place. I don't at all mean this in a disparaging way, since, as I said in my last lecture, the humanities and humanism are constitutively in need of revision, rethinking and revitalization. Once they mummify into tradition, they cease to be what they really are and become instruments of veneration and repression.

As I said a moment ago, "crisis" is the watchword, and, since it is clear that the humanities have in fact stumbled on and endured despite "the crisis," we are entitled to wonder whether what we seem to have here is a case of crying wolf over and over again. I don't mean to be supercilious, however; in the years between the end of World War II and the present, humanism in the United States has indeed undergone not just a lingering crisis but a major transformation. We are perhaps just beginning to feel an uneasiness that the usual tactic—speaking about going back to humanistic values, great texts and authors, and so on—is not as convincing as it once was and probably ought to be scuttled for the time being.

There is, I think, a genuinely alternative and more interesting argument, which I shall get to a bit later on. But for the time being, I'd like to devote myself to showing that, indeed, changes have taken place, sometimes silently and usually without getting the consideration due them. There have been changes in the very bases of what humanism and humanistic practice have been for quite a long time in the United States and elsewhere. In my first chapter, I characterized this older practice as generally Arnoldian: the changes that have overtaken this Arnoldianism are so deep, however, as to have made Arnold's residual influence more or less negligible. All the while, I shall also be saying that many of us believe, with Arnold and T. S. Eliot, that we must in some perhaps almost instinctual way continue to hold on to a wonderfully stable order of great works of art whose sustaining power means a great deal to each of us in his or her own way.

Simply to ignore the major change in the world and press on as before is, I know, one alternative and, ostrichlike, will continue to have its attractions, especially to someone like myself, who has written warmly about lost causes and has been congenitally involved with them for most of his life. In this case, however, having at the same time already persuaded myself to give up being an ostrich, I am eager to convince my reader that evading reality and fading sentimentally back into a nostalgic past is actually less workable and far less interesting—on unimpeachably humanistic grounds—than dealing with the problem rationally and systematically.

In this chapter I shall talk about the changed bases for humanistic work in the worldly and historical situation in which, as Americans, we find ourselves. In the next lecture, I shall show that the only immensely useful way to grapple with this new context is a return to a philological-interpretive model that is older and more widely based than the one that has prevailed in America since the introduction of humanistic study in the American university 150 years ago. This perhaps is sounding curiouser and curiouser, like Alice saying tearfully that she'll stay where she is until she's somebody else, but I ask the reader's forbearance for the time being.

There seems to have been a major change in the American educational psyche after World War II and the beginning of the Cold War. The fact is that the United States emerged from the good war, as it has been called, with a new awareness of its global power and, just as importantly, with a sense that it had only one major competitor for world dominance, with which, in an almost missionary-like way, it was obligated to contend. It is possible that the whole ponderously Manichean structure of the Cold War was a transmutation of a lingering earlier sense of American exceptionalism and the famous errand into the wilderness that some colonial historians have argued, to my mind unconvincingly, was essential to the formation of American identity. This sense of things was never more rhetorically acute than thirteen years after the end of the World War II, when the Soviet Union launched Sputnik in 1957, and the sense of competitive angst in "the best and the brightest" continued to build toward the Cuban missile crisis, the early years of the Vietnam War, and the l965 Indonesian upheavals, to say nothing of various Latin American, African, and Middle Eastern crises. This Cold War cultural tension is alluded to more or less routinely in every one of the conferences and composite books about the humanities that I have looked at and, nearly as frequently, in the writings of individual scholars and critics. In the 1950 Wisconsin colloquy mentioned earlier, Clark K. Kuebler, for instance, begins his contribution as follows:

> It has become uncomfortably clear that the world is in the throes of an ideological war, a war of which World War II was only another phase. We are battling over ideas and ideals; and, as we battle, we realize more and more that what a man believes in, he is and does. "Character is destiny." In fighting for democracy as opposed to totalitarianism in any form, we are involved in a struggle, which is only superficially one of politics and economics; fundamentally, it is one of values. And, ironically, the values believed in by the totalitarians are all too clear, while the values held to by believers in democracy are all too vague.

The touch of self-flagellation in Kuebler's speech had a far tougher parallel in what we now know about U.S.-government involvement in cultural politics through such agencies as the Congress of Cultural Freedom. In a powerfully argued and documented recent book (*Who Paid the Piper? The CIA and the Cultural Cold War*), the British journalist Frances Stonor Saunders gives plentiful evidence that the almost 200 million dollars spent by the CIA to subsidize innumerable humanistic and academic conferences, journals like *Encounter, Der Monat*, and *Partisan Review*, prizes, art exhibitions, concerts, musical competitions, and many individual scholars, writers, and intellectuals, had a profound effect on the kind of cultural work that was produced and the kind of activity carried on in the name of freedom and humanistic activity. I don't want to be misunderstood: the CIA did not run cultural life. Nonetheless, as it promoted and participated in a worldwide competition between freedom and totalitarianism, so naturally alluded to by Kuebler, there is good reason to assume that much of what was done and funded ideologically in the name of freedom, democratic values, and fighting communist totalitarianism, contributed significantly to humanistic praxis. It provided at least some of the overarching carapace and numerous programs and occasions for the promotion of humanism. Even so cerebral and subtle an analyst of poetry as R. P. Blackmur, probably the greatest critical explicator the United States has produced, made an early alliance with the Rockefeller Foundation, not only to finance his remarkable series of Princeton seminars (whose members included figures such as Erich Auerbach, Jacques Maritain, and Thomas Mann), but also to take several trips to the Third World in order, among other things, to gauge the depth of American influence there.

What Saunders does not note in her book, however, is that the contestatory and sometimes implicitly nationalistic, even patriotic mood of the times was not entirely due to the Cold War, just as surely as it was a result of the fundamental epistemology of modern culture and the humanities, which seems to necessitate a recasting of their situation in terms of new threats to every succeeding generation. In other words, the Cold War was part of an overall pattern in which such threats to humanistic culture seem to be ingrained in the very nature of thought about the human situation in general: the regretful last line of Cavafy's splendid poem "Waiting for the Barbarians," suggests, in its lapidary irony, how useful a hostile Other is in such circumstances—"they were, those people, a kind of solution."

Recall too that Matthew Arnold's *Culture and Anarchy*, surely the most famous modern defense of high culture and high humanism ever written, seizes on the Hyde Park riots, the agitation around the Second Reform Bill, and, as Gauri Viswanathan has shown, the continuing colonial crisis in India and Ireland, to make its arguments in favor of the best that has been known and thought in terms of the basic opposition embalmed in the book's title, though one could substitute "versus" for "and." The shadow of the Cold War, therefore, to say nothing of unending rhetoric about freedom versus totalitarianism, not unexpectedly sat over humanistic praxis for at least two generations.

Humanism as protective or even defensive nationalism is, I believe, a mixed blessing for its sometimes ideological ferocity and triumphalism, although it is sometimes inevitable. In a colonial setting, for example, the revival of the suppressed languages and cultures, the attempts at national assertion through cultural tradition and glorious ancestors (Yeats's poetry as part of the Irish literary revival in the face of British rule is a case in point), and the insistence in scholarship on the preeminence of the great national classics—these are explainable and understandable. For contemporary Palestinians, as another example here will attest, the role of bardic poetry and, alongside it, the emergence of a national style in matters of humanistic scholarship and political analysis in fields like history, the study of folklore and oral tradition, the (hitherto unsuccessful) efforts to establish a national museum and library, and making Palestinian literature a requirement of school curricula, the alternative has been national effacement, national obliteration. But in cultures where nationalism succeeded in gaining national independence, there has also been the danger of an inflamed xenophobia that is intolerant in the extreme, especially when it lives on in the form of civil war and religious strife. All cultures have this as a latent tendency, which is one reason why I have connected the humanities directly with the critical sense of inquiry, rather than with what Julien Benda calls the mobilization of collective passions.

Certainly the NDEA Title IX program that turned language study in post-Sputnik America into a concern of national interest had something very directly to do with the urgent sense of outside-threat inflections reflected in many discussions of the humanities, even though not every act or scholarly enterprise showed it. We know that area studies, for instance, anthropology, history, sociology, political science, and language studies, to name only a few fields, were underwritten by Cold War concerns. This is not to say that everyone who worked in those fields was in the pay of the CIA, but it is to say that an underlying consensus about knowledge began to emerge that was scarcely visible then but has, retrospectively, become increasingly evident. This was quite true of the academic humanities where, as many commentators have shown, the notion of nonpolitical aesthetic analysis was meant as a barrier against the overt politicization of art that was said to be conspicuously evident in socialist realism.

And so the idea of the disengaged humanist whose area of expertise (itself a deeply ideological and, in the knowledge-related world, highly capitalized and institutionalized notion) was culture and, within culture, the study of, say, Milton or eighteenth-century neoclassicism or romantic poetry, gained a great deal of currency in the second half of the twentieth century. I was formed as a scholar and teacher of Western literature inside the shelter of this idea. At the very least, as I can recall with considerable clarity, it kept in place an extremely apolitical and rigid, even mechanical conception of literary history. There were successive periods, major authors, leading concepts that were amenable to research, to comparative analysis, and to thematic organization, but never to a radical examination of the ideology of the field itself. That was the way I was intellectually formed, and I don't want to imply anything but gratitude for the access to libraries, learned professors, and great institutions it offered me: there were definite things to learn, a huge amount of literature to be responsible for, and a well-organized hierarchical system to internalize and respect (major authors, continuities, and genres such as the novel, the lyric, and the drama, minor authors, movements, styles, and then the whole world of secondary scholarship).

The important notion, however, is that none of this was meant to be intellectually rigorous or systematic, since humanistic education was in the end all about a certain unstated idea of freedom that was believed to derive from a noncoercive, albeit triumphalist attitude towards our supposedly "better" reality. The climax and at the same time the strangely exasperated transcendental expression of this elaborate, not to say febrile machine was the publication in 1957 of Northrop Frye's summa, *The Anatomy of Criticism*. Its purpose was nothing less than an attempted Blakean-Jungean synthesis of the humanistic system organized into a mini-life-world with its own seasons, cycles, rituals, heroes, social classes, and utopian pastoral as well as urban settings. The core of Frye's amazing invention is what Blake called the human divine, a macrocosmic man doing service as the embodiment of a Judeo-Christian Eurocentric norm, all of it with reference to precisely the same literature that, for all their differences, Arnold, the New Humanists, and Eliot favored, though without the invidious rankings that crippled their findings and rendered their schemes unpleasantly elitist. Frye too claimed to be talking about literature humanistically, liberally, and democratically, as his admirers Angus Fletcher and Geoffrey Hartman emphasized.

The schemata, traditions, and continuities proposed by Arnold, Eliot, and Frye, and by their various followers, had many features in common: all were almost entirely Eurocentric, masculine, and driven by genres, or archetypes as Frye called them. Neither the novel nor the drama, for example, according to the rigid terms of this system, had very much to do with the specific historical, political, and economic (to say nothing of ideological) circumstances that also enabled their rising. Certainly the notion that there was a genre called "women's" or "minority" writing never entered Frye's system, nor that of the humanistic world of agency and work whose quietly militant conclusions he represented. Nationalism did not play a role, for instance, in the narratives Frye discussed, and the power of institutions like the monarchy, the treasury, the colonial companies, and land-settlement agencies were not given notice at all, neither in Shakespeare nor in Jane Austen nor in Ben Jonson nor most impressively in all the great writing by and about Ireland, from Spenser to Yeats, Wilde, Joyce, and Shaw, whose core concerns are precisely the definition and ownership of the land itself. The struggle over property, whether that of the landed estates, the American frontier, or the colonial regions, was simply excluded both by Frye and his contemporaries and the New Critics before him, even though it is noted, and even made the center of the work often enough by Blake himself, to say nothing of Dickens, Jane Austen, Cooper, Melville, Twain, and all the other authors whose works constitute the classics. "Race" was a word never mentioned by Frye. Slavery, as having had something to do with maintaining the kingdom of heaven on earth, received no attention, nor did the literature of slaves, the poor, or minorities.

What Frye did was superbly ingenious, though, and it will stand as a monument not to the scientific humanistic criticism he believed he was formulating once and for all, but as the last synthesis of a worldview in the American humanities that has been slowly dissolving ever since. I'm not sure whether it constituted a "liberal" world view underpinned by enormous prosperity and power, or whether it was properly speaking an ornament to prettify a sordid actuality. But let me return directly to the changes. Take two elements that play a significant but relatively unstressed role in the humanistic worldview that I've been describing: one is the idea that literature exists within an assumed national context; the second is the assumption that literary objects, lyrics, tragedies, or novels, exist in some sort of stable or at least consistently identifiable form. Both of these assumptions are now profoundly unsettled. Thus it seems to many of us today that considerable doubt and inadequacy surround the notion that a Wordsworthian ode emanates from eighteenth-century English literature or that it is the work of a solitary genius or that it has the status of a work of art, removed and distinct from other works such as pamphlets, letters, parliamentary debates, religious or legal tracts, and so on. Such doubts and the corresponding scholarship about communities, affiliations between writers and social formations, classes, historical structures, and the relationships between knowledge and power, have eroded national and aesthetic frameworks, limits, and boundaries almost completely. Consequently, the notions of author, work, and nation are not the dependable categories they once were. This is by no means to deny the existence of authors and works (only a fool would do so), but rather it is to complicate and vary their modes of existence so much as to cast doubt on any assurance we may have when we say with reassuring finality, for instance, that Wordsworth wrote X or Y, and that is that. Neither Wordsworth nor X nor Y as ideas can be exempt from skeptical scrutiny as to limits, explanatory efficacy, and knowable depth.

Even the idea of the imagination, a central tenet in all literary humanism at least since the middle of the eighteenth century, has undergone an almost Copernican transformation. The original explanatory power of the term has been modified by such alien and transpersonal concepts as ideology, the unconscious, structures of feeling, anxiety, and many others. In addition, acts of imagination, which used to stand alone and do all the work of what we may still call creation, have become reformulated in terms that include performatives, constructions, and discursive statements; in some cases these seem to have entirely dissolved the possibility of agency, whereas in others, agency, or the will, no longer has the sovereign authority or plays the role it once did. Even to speak of a work of literature as a creation is, for some critics, to presume too much, since "creation" carries too many connotations of miraculous conception and completely autonomous activity to be allowed the explanatory sway it once had. This is not to say, of course, that any of these challenged words and ideas have simply disappeared—they have not—but they often seem to provoke so many doubts and suspicions as to render them all but unusable.

I believe they are still useable, since the core of humanistic effort and achievement always rests on individual effort and originality of one kind or another. Nevertheless, it would be folly, I think, to pretend that writers, musicians, and painters do their work as if on a tabula rasa: the world is already so heavily inscribed not only with the work of past writers and artists but also with the tremendous wash of information and discourse that crowds around one's individual consciousness today, with cyberspace and an enormous archive of material assaulting one's senses from all sides. Michel Foucault and Thomas Kuhn have done a considerable service by reminding us in their work that, whether we are aware of it or not, paradigms and epistemes have a throughgoing hold on fields of thought and expression, a hold that inflects if it does not shape the nature of the individual utterance. The mechanisms involved in the preservation of knowledge in archives, the rules governing the formation of concepts, the vocabulary of expressive languages, the various systems of dissemination: these all enter to some extent the individual mind and influence it so that we can no longer say with absolute confidence where individuality ends and the public realm begins. Nevertheless, my contention here is that it is the mark of humanistic scholarship, reading, and interpretation to be able to disentangle the usual from the unusual and the ordinary from the extraordinary in aesthetic works as well as in the statements made by philosophers, intellectuals, and public figures. Humanism is, to some extent, a resistance to *idées reçues*, and it offers opposition to every kind of cliché and unthinking language. I will have more to say about this later, but here I just want to insist that far from humanistic effort being determined (or for that matter predetermined) by socioeconomic circumstances, it is the dialectic of opposites, of antagonism between those circumstances and the individual humanist that is of the deepest interest, not conformity or identity.

Still, it is worth saying more about the important shift in perspective that has resulted from the changed relationship between the private and public spheres. Even such wildly popular authors in their own time as Dickens and Shakespeare were studied by academic humanists until recently as furnishing readers—the reader is a central feature of all humanism—with essentially private, inward, meditative experiences of a rarified spiritual nature not readily available to public scrutiny. Along with the very notion of privacy itself, all that is now in a state of contention, to say the least. A new, bustling traffic between private and public sphere, one interpenetrating and modifying the other, has shifted the ground almost totally, so that, as Arjun Appadurai argues in his book *Modernity at Large*, forces such as migration and electronic mediation have acquired shaping roles in the production of contemporary culture and within education, where, just to mention some of the central changes he analyzes, diasporic communities replace settled ones, new mythographies and fantasies energize as well as deaden the mind, and consumption on a new scale animates markets all across the globe. The reception of the humanistic work, who reads it, when, and for what purpose—all these are questions that crowd around and all but dispel any pristine or ecstatic state of aesthetic attention.

My own classes and students at Columbia have changed enormously from the mostly white males I first taught in

1963 to the multiethnic and multilingual men and women who are my students today. It is a fact universally acknowledged that, whereas the humanities used to be the study of classic texts informed by ancient Greek and Roman and Hebrew cultures, a now much more variegated audience of truly multicultural provenance is demanding, and getting, attention paid to a whole slew of formerly neglected or unheard of peoples and cultures that have encroached on the uncontested space formerly occupied by European cultures. And even the privileges accorded to entities such as ancient Greece or Israel have been subjected to, on the whole, salutary revisions that have considerably diminished their convenience as original. Whereas Attic Greece had until recently been seen as an Aryan stronghold from which all that was white and uncontaminated in European culture subsequently flowed, it has now been inextricably involved in its history with African and Semitic peoples; similarly ancient Israel is gradually being reintroduced by some biblical scholars as only one, and by no means the dominant, element in the complex intermingling of races and peoples that is the history of a post–Iron Age, multicultural Palestine. I shall say more about the consequences of these complicating aspects of contemporary American humanism a little later on.

For scholars and teachers of my generation who were educated in what was an essentially Eurocentric mode, the landscape and topography of humanistic study have therefore been altered dramatically and, I think, irreversibly. Whereas T. S. Eliot, Lukacs, Blackmur, Frye, Williams, Leavis, Kenneth Burke, Cleanth Brooks, I. A. Richards, and Rene Wellek—to cite a few authoritative and familiar names almost at random, names that are in fact often far apart politically and personally—all inhabited a mental and aesthetic universe that was linguistically, formally, and epistemologically grounded in the European and North Atlantic (E. P. Thompson called it the

Natopolitan) world of the classics, the church, and empire, in their traditions, languages, and masterworks, along with a whole ideological apparatus of canonicity, synthesis, centrality and consciousness. All this has now been replaced by a much more varied and complex world with many contradictory, even antinomian and antithetical currents running within it. The Eurocentric vision had already been drafted for a more and more discredited use in the Cold War, and, as I said a moment ago, for my generation of humanistically trained scholars of the 1950s and 1960s, it seemed to sit there reassuringly in the background, while in the foreground, in classes, scholarly discourse, and public discussion, humanism was rarely reflected on in a searching way, but rather continued in its grandly unthinking Arnoldian way.

The end of the Cold War coincided with a number of other changes that the culture wars of the 1980s and 1990s mirrored: the antiwar and antisegregation struggles at home, the cumulative emergence of an impressive set of dissenting voices—building on rediscovered older ones—as heard and seen all across the world in historical, anthropological, feminist, minority, and other marginalized and oppositional sectors of the main branches of humanism and the social sciences. All this contributed to the slow seismic change in humanistic perspective that is ours today at the beginning of the twenty-first century. To take one instance: African American studies as a new, albeit scandalously delayed or suppressed-in-its-appearance humanistic field represented in the academy, has fortunately had the capacity to do two things simultaneously: first, it called into question the formulaic, perhaps even hypocritical universalism of classical Eurocentric humanistic thought, and, second, it established its own relevance and urgency as a major component of American humanism in our time. And these two changes in turn revealed how the whole notion of humanism, which had for so long done without the historical experiences of African Americans, women, and disadvantaged and marginalized groups, was revealed to have been undergirded by a working notion of national identity that was, to say the least, highly edited and abridged, indeed restricted to a small group that was thought to be representative of the whole society but was in fact missing large segments of it, segments whose inclusion would actually be truer to the ceaseless flux and sometimes unpleasant violence that reflects the immigrant and multicultural realities of America.

The year 1992, the five hundredth anniversary of Columbus's appearance in the Americas, was the occasion for an often bracing debate about his achievements as well as the various dire ravages that his presence here symbolized. I know that such debates are lamented by traditional humanists as violating the sanctity of a supposedly spiritual domain, but their argument only demonstrates once again that, for them, theology, not history, is the presiding authority over humanism. One should not forget Walter Benjamin's dictum that every document of civilization is also a document of barbarism. Humanists should be especially able to see exactly what that means.

For that is where humanism is today: it is being required to take account of what, in its high Protestant mode, it had either repressed or deliberately ignored. New historians of the classical humanism of the early Renaissance (e.g., David Wallace) have at last begun to examine the circumstances in which iconic figures like Petrarch and Boccaccio lauded the "human" and yet were not even stirred into opposition to the Mediterranean slave trade. And after decades of celebrating the American "founding fathers" and heroic national figures, there is at last some attention being paid to their dubious connections to slavery, the elimination of the Native Americans, and the exploitation of nonlandowning, nonmale populations. There is a straight line between these once-occluded figures in the carpet and Frantz Fanon's comment that "the Graeco-Roman statue [of humanism] is crumbling in the colonies." More than ever before, it is true to say that the new generation of humanist scholars is more attuned than any before it to the non-European, genderized, decolonized, and decentered energies and currents of our time. But, one is entitled to ask, what does that in fact really mean? Principally it means situating critique at the very heart of humanism, critique as a form of democratic freedom and as a continuous practice of questioning and of accumulating knowledge that is open to, rather than in denial of, the constituent historical realities of the post–Cold War world, its early colonial formation, and the frighteningly global reach of the last remaining superpower of today.

I'm not in a position here, nor is this the time, to try to provide a sketch of what those realities are, except to say that if a nationalistic or Eurocentric humanism served well enough in the past, it is of no use now for many of the reasons I have outlined already. Ours is a society whose historical and cultural identity cannot be confined to one tradition or race or religion. Even countries like Sweden and Italy, which had seemed homogenous for centuries, are now permanently altered by the huge waves of migrants, expatriates, and refugees that have become the single most important human reality of our time the world over, but which has been the central demographic and cultural fact of the United States since its inception. What this transformation means is nothing less than that nativist cultural traditions that pretend to authenticity and aboriginal priority can now be recognized as the great patently false and misleading fundamentalist ideology of the time. Those still clinging to it are the falsifiers and reductivists, the fundamentalists and deniers, whose doctrines must be criticized for what they leave out, denigrate, demonize, and dehumanize on presumably humanistic grounds. With so irreversible a mixture of human peoples all around us, part of us, it must be the case that to some extent we are all outsiders and, to a slightly lesser but almost equal extent, insiders simultaneously. Everyone belongs to some identifiable non-American (that is, either immigrant or pre-U.S.) native tradition, and at the same time—and this is the peculiar richness of America—everyone is an outsider to some other identity or tradition adjacent to one's own. Taken seriously and literally, as indeed it must be, this factor alone allows us to dismiss out of hand the notion that insiders, whether they be minorities or disadvantaged victims or members of an ascendant Eurocentric cultural tradition have an unassailable right to represent some historical experience or truth which is uniquely their own by virtue mainly of primordial membership in the group. No, we must say by way of critical rejoinder, it cannot be true that only members of a certain group should be permitted the last (or for that matter the only) word when it comes to expressing or representing that group's experience, which, after all, is part of the general American experience that, despite its undoubtedly special, irreducibly individual core, shares in the same worldly context as all the others.

The key word here is "worldly," a notion I have always used to denote the real historical world from whose circumstances none of us can in fact ever be separated, not even in theory. I recall quite emphatically making a similar set of points in my book *Orientalism*, when I criticized the representations of the Orient and Orientals by Western experts. My critique was premised on the flawed nature of all representations and how they are intimately tied up with worldliness, that is, with power, position, and interests. This required saying explicitly that my work was not intended as a defense of the real Orient or that it even made the case that a real Orient existed. I certainly held no brief for the purity of some representations against others, and I was quite specific in suggesting that no process of converting experience into expression could be free of contamination. It was already and necessarily contaminated by its involvement with power, position, and interests, whether it was a victim of them or not. Worldliness—by which I mean at a more precise cultural level that all texts and all representations were *in* the world and subject to its numerous heterogeneous realities—assured contamination and involvement, since in all cases the history and presence of various other groups and individuals made it impossible for anyone to be free of the conditions of material existence.

Nowhere is this more true than for the American humanist today, whose proper role, I cannot stress strongly enough, is not to consolidate and affirm one tradition over all the others. It is rather to open them all, or as many as possible, to each other, to question each of them for what it has done with the others, to show how in this polyglot country in particular many traditions have interacted and—more importantly—can continue to interact in peaceful ways, ways never easy to find but nonetheless discoverable also in other multicultural societies like the former Yugoslavia or Ireland or the Indian subcontinent or the Middle East. In other words, American humanism, by virtue of what is available to it in the normal course of its own context and historical reality, is already in a state of civic coexistence, and, to the prevailing worldview disseminated by U.S. officialdom—especially in its dealings with the world outside America—humanism provides little short of stubborn, and secular, intellectual resistance.

Among these multicultural societies, there are, it is true, all sorts of inequities and disparities, but each national identity is fundamentally capable of acknowledging and coping with these problems if there are suitable models of coexistence (as opposed to partition) provided by humanists whose mission,

I believe, is precisely to provide such models. I am not speaking of domestication, of tokenism, or of polite civility. One such model for literary humanistic study is going to be the specific subject of my next chapter. The point I want to make here is that what I have in mind is not a lazy or laissez-faire feel-good multiculturalism. That frankly means absolutely nothing to me as it is usually discussed. I have in mind a far more rigorous intellectual and rational approach that, as I have already suggested, draws on a rather exact notion of what it means to read philologically in a worldly and integrative, as distinct from separating or partitioning, mode and, at the same time, to offer resistance to the great reductive and vulgarizing us-versus-them thought patterns of our time.

Doubtless there are many negative examples afforded us not only by our history but by the general tenor of modern experience all over the world. Of these negative models, whose wake is strewn with ruin, waste, and human suffering unlimited, three in particular deserve accentuation: nationalism, religious enthusiasm, and the exclusivism that derives from what Adorno refers to in his work as identitarian thought. All three are opposed to the mutuality of cultural pluralism that the U.S. constitution and its very founding ideas actively promote. Nationalism gives rise not only to the affirmative mischief of exceptionalism and the various paranoid doctrines of "un-Americanism" by which our modern history is so unfortunately disfigured, but also to narratives of patriotic sovereignty and separateness that are inordinately bellicose about enemies, the clash of civilizations, manifest destiny, "our" natural superiority, and, inevitably (as now), to policies of arrogant interventionism in politics the world over, so that, alas, in places like Iraq, the United States today is synonymous with a very harsh inhumanity and with policies whose results are particularly and, I would say, even perniciously destructive. This sort of American nationalism would be comic if it were not actually so utterly devastating and even tragic in its consequences.

Religious enthusiasm is perhaps the most dangerous of threats to the humanistic enterprise, since it is patently anti-secular and antidemocratic in nature, and, in its monotheistic forms as a kind of politics, is by definition about as intoler-antly inhumane and downright unarguable as can be. Invidi-ous commentary about the world of Islam after 9/11 has made it popular wisdom that Islam is by nature a violent, intolerant religion, much given to raving fundamentalism and suicidal terrorism. There have been no end of "experts" and evangelists repeating the same rubbish, aided and abetted by discredited Orientalists like Bernard Lewis. It is a sign of the intellectual and humanistic poverty of the times that such patent propaganda (in the literal sense of the word) has gained such currency and, even more disastrously, that it is carried on without the slightest reference to Christian, Jewish, and Hindu fundamentalism, which, as extremist political ideolo-gies, have been at least as bloody and disastrous as Islam. All these enthusiasms belong essentially to the same world, feed off one another, emulate and war against one another schiz-ophrenically, and—most seriously—are as ahistorical and as intolerant as one another. Surely it must be a major part of the humanistic vocation to keep fully rounded secular perspec-tive, not to follow the trimmers and the neutrals (those who Dante calls "coloro che visser sanza infamia e sanza lodo") who attack the foreign demons while winking complaisantly at their own. Religious fanaticism is religious fanaticism no matter who advocates or practices it. It is inexcusable to take an "ours is better than yours" attitude toward it.

By "exclusivism," I mean that avoidable narrowing of vision that sees in the past only self-flattering narratives that deliberately filter out not just the achievements of other groups but in a sense even their fructifying presence. America,

Palestine, Europe, the West, Islam, and all the other "big" names of our time: these are composite, partly constructed and partly invented but heavily invested entities. To turn them into limited clubs for select members is to do what I suggested earlier has frequently been done to humanism in our time. Even in the hotly contested worlds of politics and religion, cultures are intertwined and can only be disentangled from each other by mutilating them. So let's not hear talk of the clash of civilizations or the conflict of cultures: these are the worst sort of us–versus–them structures, whose net result is always to impoverish and narrow vision, only very rarely to enlighten and further understanding.

In both the humanities and the social sciences, the nub of these limiting models is very often Eurocentrism, a besetting problem that is about as inappropriate to humanistic practice in the United States as it is possible to be, if only because such a distortion of our social and historical realities today is little short of a disaster. Immanuel Wallerstein has, over the last couple of years, been writing a sustained intellectual critique of Eurocentrism that serves my purposes here very well, so let me draw for a time on him. In doing so, I shall elide the social sciences that Wallerstein speaks about with the humanities, since the problems in the latter are exactly the same as in the former:

> Social science [and, I would argue, the modern humanities] emerged in response to European problems [in basically five countries, France, Great Britain, Germany, Italy, and the United States] at a point in history when Europe dominated the whole world-system. It was virtually inevitable that its choice of subject matter, its theorizing, its methodology, and its epistemology all reflected the constraints of the crucible within which it was born. However, in the period since 1945, the decolonization of Asia and Africa, along with the sharply accentuated political consciousness of the non-European world every-

> where, has affected the world of knowledge just as much as it
> has affected the politics of the world system. One major such
> difference, today and indeed for some thirty years now at least,
> is that the 'Eurocentrism' of social sciences [and the humani-
> ties] has been under attack, severe attack. The attack is of course
> fundamentally justified, and there is no question that . . . [we]
> must overcome the Eurocentric heritage which has distorted
> [their] analyses and [their] capacity to deal with the problems
> of the contemporary world. (93–94)

I do not believe that, like the social sciences, the humanities must address or somehow solve the problems of the contemporary world. It is a matter of being able to see and
understand humanistic practice as an integral aspect and
functioning part of that world and not as an ornament or an
exercise in nostalgic retrospection. Eurocentrism blocks such
a prospect because, as Wallerstein says, its misleadingly skewed
historiography, the parochiality of its universalism, its unexamined assumptions about Western civilization, its Orientalism, and its attempts to impose a uniformly directed theory
of progress all end up by reducing, rather than expanding, the
possibility of catholic inclusiveness, of genuinely cosmopolitan or internationalist perspective, of intellectual curiosity.

Looking back at most of the twentieth-century history of
American humanism, one is obliged to say that it has been
seriously afflicted with the kind of Eurocentrism that can no
longer be allowed to remain unquestioned. Across the board,
the restrictions of basic core university courses to a small
number of translated and dutifully venerated Western masterpieces, the narrowed perspectives on what constitutes "our"
world, the obliviousness to traditions and languages that seem
to be outside respectable or approved attention—all of these
must be jettisoned or at the very least submitted to a radical
humanistic critique. For one thing, too much is known about
other traditions to believe that even humanism itself is exclu-

sively a Western practice. As a particularly telling example, take two important studies by Professor George Makdisi on the rise of humanism and the Islamic contribution to it. His studies demonstrate amply and with enormous erudition that the practices of humanism, celebrated as originating in fourteenth- and fifteenth-century Italy by authorities such as Jakob Burkhardt, Paul Oskar Kristeller, and nearly every academic historian after them, in fact began in the Muslim *madaris*, colleges, and universities of Sicily, Tunis, Baghdad, and Seville at least two hundred years earlier. And the habit of mind that occludes this wider, more complex history still persists. If I focus on the exclusions of the Islamic contributions to civilization in the West, it is obviously because I have treated the misrepresentations of Orientalism in much of my earlier work, and therefore I know something about their history and politics. But the same kind of Eurocentric exclusions are evident in Western humanistic neglect of the Indian, Chinese, African, and Japanese traditions, to name some of the more obvious examples. We now know so much about these others as in effect to explode any simple, formulaic accounts of humanism, accounts still being trotted out by reclaimers of "our" heritage or in celebrations of the Western miracle or in panegyrics to how glorious a thing is American globalization. It is little short of scandalous, for instance, that nearly every medieval studies program in our universities routinely overlooks one of the high points of medieval culture, namely, Muslim Andalusia before 1492, and that, as Martin Bernal has shown for ancient Greece, the complex intermingling of European, African, and Semitic cultures has been laundered clean of that heterogeneity so troublesome to current humanism. If we agree that essentialism is assailable, indeed profoundly vulnerable on epistemological grounds, then why does it nonetheless persist at the heart of humanism, where cultural pride of an extraordinarily uninteresting variety takes over when the labels and claims begin to seem untenable or simply false? When will we stop allowing ourselves to think of humanism as a form of smugness and not as an unsettling adventure in difference, in alternative traditions, in texts that need a new deciphering within a much wider context than has hitherto been given them?

It therefore seems to me that we must begin to rid ourselves, consciously and resolutely, of the whole complex of attitudes associated not just with Eurocentrism but with identity itself, which can no longer be tolerated in humanism as easily as it was before and during the Cold War. Taking their cue from the literature, thought, and art of our time, humanists must recognize with some alarm that the politics of identity and the nationalistically grounded system of education remain at the core of what most of us actually do, despite changed boundaries and objects of research. There is a considerable discrepancy between what we practice as humanists and what we know of the wider world as citizens and scholars. The problem is not only that our educational program still aims at a simple concept of American identity (as witness the lament for the former "unity" of American history by Arthur Schlesinger Jr.). We have also been witnessing the advent of aggressive new subspecialties, mostly centered on the academic study of postmodern identities. These have been displaced from the worldly context into the academy—and therefore denatured and depoliticized—imperiling that sense of a collective human history as grasped in some of the global patterns of dependence and interdependence sketched by Appadurai, Wallerstein, and, if I may mention my own effort, in the last chapter of my *Culture and Imperialism*. Would it be possible to introduce a *modernist* theory and practice of reading and interpreting the part to the whole in a such a way as neither to deny the specificity of the individual experience in and of an aesthetic work nor to rule out the validity of a projected, putative, or implied sense of the whole? It is that possibility which I should like to treat in my next chapter.

References

Appadurai, Arjun. *Modernity at Large: Cultural Dimensions of Globalization.* Minneapolis: University of Minnesota Press, 1996.

Cavafy, Constantine P. "Waiting for the Barbarians." In *Before Time Could Change Them: The Complete Poems of Constantine P. Cavafy.* Trans. Theoharis Constantine Theoharis. New York: Harcourt, 2001.

Frye, Northrop. *The Anatomy of Criticism.* Princeton: Princeton University Press, 1957.

Saunders, Frances Stonor. *Who Paid the Piper? The CIA and the Cultural Cold War.* London: Granta, 1999.

Viswanathan, Gauri. *Masks of Conquest: Literary Study and British Rule in India.* New York: Columbia University Press, 1989.

Wallerstein, Immanuel. "Eurocentrism and its Avatars." *New Left Review* 226 (November/December 1997): 93–107.

3

THE RETURN TO PHILOLOGY

PHILOLOGY IS JUST ABOUT THE LEAST WITH-IT, LEAST SEXY, and most unmodern of any of the branches of learning associated with humanism, and it is the least likely to turn up in discussions about humanism's relevance to life at the beginning of the twenty-first century. But that rather discouraging thought shall have to sit for a while, as I try to move into my subject with my head held high and, I hope, your endurance strong. I suppose that it would help lower resistance to the otherwise perhaps unattractive idea of philology as a mustily antiquarian discipline to begin by mentioning that perhaps the most radical and intellectually audacious of all Western thinkers during the past 150 years, Nietzsche, was and always considered himself first and foremost a philologist. That should immediately dispel any vestigial notion of philology as a form of reactionary learning, the kind embodied in the character of Dr, Casaubon in George Eliot's *Middlemarch*—sterile, ineffectual, and hopelessly irrelevant to life.

Philology is, literally, the love of words, but as a discipline it acquires a quasi-scientific intellectual and spiritual prestige at various periods in all of the major cultural traditions, including the Western and the Arabic-Islamic traditions that have framed my own development. Suffice it to recall briefly that in the Islamic tradition, knowledge is premised upon a philological attention to language beginning with the Koran, the uncreated word of God (and indeed the word "Koran" itself means reading), and continuing through the emergence of scientific grammar in Khalil ibn Ahmad and Sibawayh to the rise of jurisprudence (*fiqh*) and *ijtihad* and *ta'wil*, jurisprudential hermeneutics and interpretation, respectively. Later, the study of *fiqh al lugha*, or the hermeneutics of language, emerges in Arab-Islamic culture as possessing considerable importance as a practice for Islamic learning. All these involve a detailed scientific attention paid to language as bearing within it knowledge of a kind entirely limited to what language does and does not do. There was (as I mentioned in my last chapter) a consolidation of the interpretive sciences that underlie the system of humanistic education, which was itself established by the twelfth century in the Arab universities of southern Europe and North Africa, well before its counterpart in the Christian West. Similar developments occur in the closely related Judaic tradition in Andalusia, North Africa, the Levant, and Mesopotamia. In Europe, Giambattista Vico's *New Science* (1744) launches an interpretive revolution based upon a kind of philological heroism whose results are to reveal, as Nietzsche was to put it a century and a half later, that the truth concerning human history is "a mobile army of metaphors and metonyms" whose meaning is to be unceasingly decoded by acts of reading and interpretation grounded in the shapes of words as bearers of reality, a reality hidden, misleading, resistant, and difficult. The science of reading, in other words, is paramount for humanistic knowledge.

Emerson said of language that it is "fossil poetry," or, as Richard Poirier explicates the notion, "that there are discoverable traces in language of that aboriginal power by which we invent ourselves as a unique form of nature" (135). Poirier continues:

> When Emerson says in [his essay] "Prudence" that "we write from aspiration and antagonism, as well as from experience," he means that while we aspire to say something new, the materials at hand indicate that whatever we say can be understood only if it is relatively familiar. We therefore become antagonistic to conventions of language even though we are in need of them [and need to understand how they operate, for which only an attentive philological reading can serve]. Indeed, the social and literary forms that ask for our compliance were themselves produced in resistance to conventions of an earlier time. Even in words that now seem tired or dead we can discover a desire for transformation that once infused them. Any word, in the variety and even contradictoriness of its meanings, gives evidence of earlier antagonistic uses, and it is this which encourages us to turn on them again, to change or trope them still further. (138)

A true philological reading is active; it involves getting inside the process of language already going on in words and making it disclose what may be hidden or incomplete or masked or distorted in any text we may have before us. In this view of language, then, words are not passive markers or signifiers standing in unassumingly for a higher reality; they are, instead, an integral formative part of the reality itself. And, Poirier says in an earlier essay,

> literature makes the strongest possible claims on my attention because more than any other form of art or expression it demonstrates what can be made, what can be done with something shared by everyone, used by everyone in the daily conduct of life, and something, besides, which carries most subtly

and yet measurably within itself, its vocabulary and syntax, the governing assumptions of a society's social, political, and economic arrangements. . . . But [unlike works of music, dance, paintings, or films] literature depends for its principle or essential resource on materials that it must share in an utterly gregarious way with the society at large and with its history. None can teach us so much about what words do to us and how, in turn, we might try to do something to them which will perhaps modify the order of things on which they depend for their meaning. To Literature is left the distinction that it invites the reader to a dialectical relationship to words with an intensity allowable nowhere else. (133–34)

It will be clear from all this that reading is the indispensable act, the initial gesture without which any philology is simply impossible. Poirier notes simply but elegantly that literature is words put to more complex and subtle uses, both by convention and originality, than in any other place in society. I think he is absolutely right, and so in what follows I shall preserve this notion of his, that literature provides the most heightened example we have of words in action and therefore is the most complex and rewarding—for all sorts of reasons— of verbal practices. In reflecting about this recently, I came across the astounding objection current here and there amongst professors of literature in the United States that just as there is sexism and elitism and ageism and racism, there is also something reprehensible called "readism," reading considered so seriously and naively as to constitute a radical flaw. Therefore, runs this argument, one shouldn't be taken in by reading, since to read too carefully is to be misled by structures of power and authority. I find this logic (if it is logic) quite bizarre, and if it is supposed to lead us out of slavish attitudes toward authority in a liberating way then I have to say it is, alas, yet another silly chimera. Only acts of reading done more and more carefully, as Poirier suggests, more and more attentively, more and more widely, more and more receptively and resistantly (if I may coin a word) can provide humanism with an adequate exercise of its essential worth, especially given the changed bases for humanism that I spoke about in my last lecture.

For a reader of texts to move immediately, however, from a quick, superficial reading into general or even concrete statements about vast structures of power or into vaguely therapeutic structures of salutary redemption (for those who believe that literature makes you a better person) is to abandon the abiding basis for all humanistic practice. That basis is at bottom what I have been calling philological, that is, a detailed, patient scrutiny of and a lifelong attentiveness to the words and rhetorics by which language is used by human beings who exist in history: hence the word "secular," as I use it, as well as the word "worldliness." Both of these notions allow us to take account not of eternally stable or supernaturally informed values, but rather of the changing bases for humanistic praxis regarding values and human life that are now fully upon us in the new century. Again drawing on Emerson and Poirier, I should like to argue that reading involves the contemporary humanist in two very crucial motions that I shall call reception and resistance. Reception is submitting oneself knowledgeably to texts and treating them provisionally at first as discrete objects (since this is how they are initially encountered); moving then, by dint of expanding and elucidating the often obscure or invisible frameworks in which they exist, to their historical situations and the way in which certain structures of attitude, feeling, and rhetoric get entangled with some currents, some historical and social formulations of their context.

Only by receiving the text in all its complexity and with the critical awareness of change that I described in my last lecture can one move from the specific to the general both

integratively and synthetically. Thus a close reading of a literary text—a novel, poem, essay, or drama, say—in effect will
gradually locate the text in its time as part of a whole network
of relationships whose outlines and influence play an informing role *in* the text. And I think it is important to say that for
the humanist, the act of reading is the act therefore of first
putting oneself in the position of the author, for whom writing is a series of decisions and choices expressed in words. It
need hardly be said that no author is completely sovereign or
above the time, place, and circumstances of his or her life, so
that these, too, must be understood if one is to put oneself in
the author's position sympathetically. Thus to read an author
like Conrad, for example, is first of all to read his work as if
with the eye of Conrad himself, which is to try to understand
each word, each metaphor, each sentence as something consciously chosen by Conrad in preference to any number of
other possibilities. We know of course from looking at the
manuscripts of his works how laborious and how time-
consuming that process of composition and choice was for
him: it therefore behooves us as his readers to make a comparable effort by getting inside his language so to speak, inside
it so as to understand why he put it that way in particular, to
understand it as it was made.

Let me interrupt my argument here to go to the question
of aesthetics, since as someone whose intellectual life has been
dedicated largely to the understanding and teaching of great
works of literary and musical art, as well as to a career of social
and political engagement and commitment—the two sepa-
rately from each other—I have found that the quality of what
one reads is often as important as how and why one reads in
the first place. While I know there can be no prior agreement
among all readers as to what constitutes a work of art, there is
no doubt that part of the humanistic enterprise that I have
been discussing in these lectures departs from the notion that

every individual, whether by convention, personal circumstances and effort, or education, is able to recognize aesthetic
quality and distinction that can be felt, if not wholly understood, in the course of reading or experiencing. This is true in
every tradition that I know of—the institutions of literature,
for example, exist in all of them—and I see no point now in
trying to prove this by lengthy argument. I think it is also true
that the aesthetic as a category is, at a very profound level, to
be distinguished from the quotidian experiences of existence
that we all have. To read Tolstoy, Mahfouz, or Melville, to lis-
ten to Bach, Duke Ellington, or Elliott Carter, is to do something different from reading the newspaper or listening to the
taped music you get while the phone company or your doc-
tor puts you on hold. This is not to say, however, that journal-
ism or policy papers are to be read quickly and superficially: I
advocate attentive reading in all cases, as I shall be showing
later. But in the main, I would agree with Adorno that there
is a fundamental irreconcilability between the aesthetic and
the nonaesthetic that we must sustain as a necessary condition
of our work as humanists. Art is not simply there: it exists
intensely in a state of unreconciled opposition to the depre-
dations of daily life, the uncontrollable mystery on the bestial
floor. One can call this heightened status for art the result of
performance, of protracted elaboration (as in the structures of
a great novel or poem), of ingenious execution and insight: I
myself cannot do without the category of the aesthetic as, in
the final analysis, providing resistance not only to my own
efforts to understand and clarify and elucidate as reader, but
also as escaping the leveling pressures of everyday experience
from which, however, art paradoxically derives.

Yet this aesthetic fact by no means entails the ultimate oth-
erworldliness that, some theorists and artists have maintained,
allows the work of art to escape meaningful discussion and
historical reflection altogether. Nor, much as I am tempted by

her argument, can I go as far as Elaine Scarry in making an
equivalence between loving the beauty of art and being just.
On the contrary, as I argued in *Culture and Imperialism*, the
interesting thing about a great work is that it generates more,
rather than less complexity and becomes over time what
Raymond Williams has called a whole web of often contradictory cultural notations. Even the skillfully wrought novels
of Jane Austen, for instance, are affiliated with the circumstances of her time; this is why she makes elaborate reference
to such sordid practices as slavery and fights over property. Yet,
to repeat, her novels can never be reduced only to social,
political, historical, and economic forces but rather, are, anti-
thetically, in an unresolved dialectical relationship with them,
in a position that obviously depends on history but is not
reducible to it. For we must, I think, assume that there is
always the supervening reality of the aesthetic work without
which the kind of humanism I am talking about here really
has no essential meaning, only an instrumental one.

Call this a particular kind of faith, or as I prefer, an enabling
conviction in the enterprise of making human history: for me
it is the ground of humanistic practice and, as I said a moment
ago, the presence of the aesthetic demands the exceptional kind
of close reading and reception whose best formulation was
given, I believe, by Leo Spitzer in the form of a philological
description of very powerful immediacy. This process of reception involves what he calls fighting one's way to the unity of an
author, the spiritual etymon, by repeated readings. Spitzer
explains that the scholar-humanist-reader must be asked

> to work from the surface to the "inward life-center" of the
> work of art: first observing details about the superficial appear-
> ance of the particular work (and the "ideas" expressed by a poet
> are, also, only one of the superficial traits in a work of art); then,
> grouping these details and seeking to integrate them into a cre-
> ative principle which may have been present in the soul of the

artist; and, finally, making the return trip to all the other groups
of observations in order to find whether the "inward form"
one has tentatively constructed gives an account of the whole.
The scholar will surely be able to state, after three or four of
these "fro voyages," whether he has found the life-giving center, the sun of the solar system [which is, according to Spitzer,
the work's compositional principle]. (19)

This actually occurs, he says a bit later, when, in the act of
reading, one is "struck by a detail, followed by a conviction
that this detail is connected basically with the work of art"
(27). There is no guarantee that the making of this connection is correct, no scientific proof that it has worked. There is
only the inner faith of the humanist "in the power bestowed
on the human mind of investigating the human mind," as well
as an abiding sense that what one finds in the work is genuinely worth investigating. For this, of course, there is no
guarantee, only a deep subjective sense for which no substitute, no guidebook or authoritative source is possible. One
must make the decision oneself and take responsibility for it.
Let me continue quoting more from Spitzer:

How often, with all the theoretical experience of method
accumulated in me over the years, have I stared blankly, quite
similar to one of my beginning students, at a page that would
not yield its magic. The only way leading out of this state of
unproductivity is to read and re-read, patiently and confidently,
in an endeavor to become, as it were[,] soaked through and
through with the atmosphere of the work. And suddenly one
word, one line, [or one set of words and lines], stands out, and
we realize that, now, a relationship has been established
between the poem and us. From this point, I have usually found
that, what with other observations adding themselves to the
first, and with previous experiences of the circles intervening,
and with associations given by previous education building up
before me ... [as well as, I would add, those prior commitments

and habits that in effect make us citizens of the society we live in, insiders and outsiders both] it does not seem long until the characteristic "click" occurs, which is the indication that detail and whole have found a common denominator—which gives the etymology of the writing. And looking back on this process . . . we see indeed, that to have read is to have read, to understand is equivalent to having understood. (27)

What is tautological about this fascinating description of close reading is precisely what needs emphasis, I think. For the process of reading begins and ends in the reader, and what enables the reading is an irreducibly personal act of commitment to reading and interpreting, the gesture of reception that includes opening oneself to the text and, just as importantly, being willing to make informed statements about its meaning and what that meaning might attach itself to. Only connect, says E. M. Forster, a marvelous injunction to the chain of statements and meanings that proliferate out of close reading. This is what R. P. Blackmur calls bringing literature to performance. And Emerson saying, "Every mind must know the whole lesson for itself,—must go over the whole ground. What it does not see, what it does not live, it will not know."

It is the avoidance of this process of taking final comradely responsibility for one's reading that explains, I think, a crippling limitation in those varieties of deconstructive Derridean readings that end (as they began) in undecidability and uncertainty. To reveal the wavering and vacillation in all writing is useful up to a point, just as it may here and there be useful to show, with Foucault, that knowledge in the end serves power. But both alternatives defer for too long a declaration that the actuality of reading is, fundamentally, an act of perhaps modest human emancipation and enlightenment that changes and enhances one's knowledge for purposes other than reductiveness, cynicism, or fruitless standing aside. Of course when we read, for example, a poem by John Ashberry or a novel by

Flaubert, attention to the text is far more intense and focused that would be the case with a newspaper or magazine article about foreign or military policy. But in both instances attention in reading requires alertness and making connections that are otherwise hidden or obscured by the text, which, in the case of an article having to do with political decisions about whether to go to war, for instance, demands that as citizens we enter into the text with responsibility and scrupulous care. Otherwise, why bother at all? As for what, in the end, are the enlightening and, yes, emancipatory purposes of close reading, I shall get to them soon enough.

No one is required to imitate the inimitable Spitzer or, for that matter, that other admirable philologist who had such a profound influence on our reading of the Western classics in this country, Erich Auerbach (about whose great work *Mimesis* I shall speak in the next chapter of this book). But it is necessary to realize that close reading has to originate in critical receptivity as well as in a conviction that even though great aesthetic work ultimately resists total understanding, there is a possibility of a critical understanding that may never be completed but can certainly be provisionally affirmed. It is a truism that all readings are of course subject to later rereadings, but it is also good to remember that there can be heroic first readings that enable many others after them. Who can forget the rush of enrichment on reading Tolstoy or hearing Wagner or Armstrong, and how can one ever forget the sense of change in oneself as a result? It takes a kind of heroism to undertake great artistic efforts, to experience the shattering disorientation of "making" an *Anna Karenina*, the Missae Luba, the Taj Mahal. This is proper, I think, to the humanistic enterprise, the sense of authorial heroism as something to emulate, admire, aspire to for readers, as well as for poets, novelists, dramatists. It is not only anxiety that drives Melville, for instance, to match Shakespeare and Milton, or anxiety that spurs Robert Lowell to go on from Eliot, or anxiety that drives Stevens to outdo the audacity of the French symbolists, or anxiety in a critic such as the late Ian Watt to go beyond Leavis and Richards. There is competitiveness of course, but also admiration and enthusiasm for the job to be done that won't be satisfied until one's own road is taken after a great predecessor has first carved out a path. Much the same can and must be said about humanistic heroism of allowing oneself to experience the work with something of its primary drive and informing power. We are not scribblers or humble scribes but minds whose actions become a part of the collective human history being made all around us.

Ideally, what keeps the humanist honest is this sense of a common enterprise shared with others, an undertaking with its own built-in constraints and disciplines. I've always found an excellent paradigm for this in the Islamic tradition, so little known amongst Eurocentric scholars all too busy extolling some supposedly exclusive humanistic Western ideal. Since in Islam the Koran is the Word of God, it is therefore impossible ever fully to grasp, though it must repeatedly be read. But the fact that it is in language already makes it incumbent on readers first of all to try to understand its literal meaning, with a profound awareness that others before them have attempted the same daunting task. So the presence of others is given as a community of witnesses whose availability to the contemporary reader is retained in the form of a chain, each witness depending to some degree on an earlier one. This system of interdependent readings is called "*isnad*." The common goal is to try to approach the ground of the text, its principle or *usul*, although there must always be a component of personal commitment and extraordinary effort, called "*ijtihad*" in Arabic. (Without a knowledge of Arabic, it is difficult to know that "*ijtihad*" derives from the same root as the now notorious word *jihad*, which does not

mainly mean holy war but rather a primarily spiritual exertion on behalf of the truth.) It is not surprising that since the
fourteenth century there has been a robust struggle going on
about whether *ijtihad* is permissible, to what degree, and
within what limits. The dogmatic view of orthodox Islamic
readings argues that Ibn-Taymiyya (1263–1328 C.E.) was right
and that only *as-salaf al-salih* (pious forerunners) should be
followed, thus closing the door, as it were, on individual interpretation. But that has always been challenged, especially
since the eighteenth century, and the proponents of *ijtihad*
have by no means been routed.

As with other interpretive religious traditions, a great deal
of controversy has accrued to all these terms and their admis-
sible meanings, and perhaps I dangerously simplify or overlook
many of the arguments. But I am right in saying that at the
limits of what is permissible in any personal effort to understand a text's rhetorical and semantic structure are the requirements of jurisprudence, narrowly speaking, plus the conventions and mentalities, speaking more broadly, of an age. Law,
qanun, is what, in the public realm, governs or has hegemony
over acts of personal initiative even when freedom of expression is decently available. Responsibly, one cannot just say anything one pleases and in whichever way one may wish to say
it. This sense of responsibility and acceptability not only reins
in quite impressively what Spitzer has to say about philological induction, but also sets the limits for what Emerson and
Poirier offer: all three examples I have given, from the Arab,
philological-hermeneutic, and pragmatic American traditions,
use different terms to characterize something like conventions, semantic frameworks, and social or even political communities operating as partial constraints on what would otherwise be an out-of-control subjective frenzy, which is what
Swift parodies mercilessly in *A Tale of a Tub*.

Between the abiding enactment of a rigorous commitment to reading for meaning—and not simply for discursive structures and textual practices, which is not to say those are not important—and the requirements of formulating that meaning as it contributes actively to enlightenment and emancipation, there is a considerable space for the exercise of humanistic energy. A recent study by David Harlan correctly laments in its contents and title—*The Degradation of American History*—the slow dissipation of gravity and commitment in the writing of American history and theory. I do not agree with his somewhat sentimental exceptionalist conclusions about what America should be learning from its own history, but his diagnosis of the currently depressed state of academic writing is an accurate one. He contends that the influence of antifoundationalism, discourse analysis, automatized and tokenized relativism, and professionalism, among other orthodoxies, has denatured and defanged the historian's mission. Much the same applies, I believe, in humanistic literary practice, where a new dogmatism has separated some literary professionals not only from the public sphere but from other professionals who don't use the same jargon. The alternatives seem now to be quite impoverishing: either become a technocratic deconstructionist, discourse analyst, new historicist, and so on, or retreat into a nostalgic celebration of some past state of glory associated with what is sentimentally evoked as humanism. What is missing altogether is some intellectual, as opposed to a merely technical, component to humanistic practice that might restore it to a place of relevance in our time. This is what I am trying to do here, that is, to escape the impoverishing dichotomy.

Enter at last the notion of resistance. I see no way at all of introducing resistance without the prior discussion of reception in the various ways I have just described, however inadequately and telegraphically: that process of reading and philological reception is the irreducible core. To recapitulate briefly: Reception is based on *ijtihad*, close reading, hermeneutic induction, and it entails troping the general language further in one's own critical language with a full recognition that the work of art in question remains at a necessary final remove, unreconciled and in a state of integral wholeness that one has tried to comprehend or impose. But the process does not stop there by any means. For if, as I believe, there is now taking place in our society an assault on thought itself, to say nothing of democracy, equality, and the environment, by the dehumanizing forces of globalization, neoliberal values, economic greed (euphemistically called the free market), as well as imperialist ambition, the humanist must offer alternatives now silenced or unavailable through the channels of communication controlled by a tiny number of news organizations.

We are bombarded by prepackaged and reified representations of the world that usurp consciousness and preempt democratic critique, and it is to the overturning and dismantling of these alienating objects that, as C. Wright Mills put it so correctly, the intellectual humanist's work ought to be devoted. It is still very fortunately the case, however, that the American university remains the one public space available to real alternative intellectual practices: no other institution like it on such a scale exists anywhere else in the world today, and I for one am immensely proud to have been a part of it for the longest and better part of my life. University humanists are in an exceptionally privileged position in which to do their work, but it is not simply as academic professionals or experts that their advantage lies. Rather, the academy—with its devotion to reflection, research, Socratic teaching, and some measure of skeptical detachment—allows one freedom from the deadlines, the obligations to an importunate and exigent employer, and the pressures to produce on a regular basis, that afflict so many experts in our policy-think-tank

riddled age. Not the least valuable thing about the reflection
and thought that takes place in a university is that one has
time to do it.

One issue that comes up directly is the matter of what language to use in the work of resistance, what idiom, what
manner of addressing one's students, colleagues, fellow citizens. There has been considerable debate in the academic and
popular media about so-called good and bad writing. My
own pragmatic answer to the problem is simply to avoid jargon that only alienates a potentially wide constituency. True,
as Judith Butler has argued, the prepackaged style of what is
considered acceptable prose risks concealing the ideological
presuppositions it is based on; she has cited Adorno's difficult
syntax and thorny mode of expression as a precedent for
eluding, even defeating the smooth papering-over of injustice
and suffering by which discourse covers its complicity with
political malfeasance. Unfortunately, Adorno's poetic insights
and dialectical genius are in very short supply even among
those who try to emulate his style; as Sartre said in another
context, Valéry was a petit bourgeois, but not every petit
bourgeois is a Valéry. Not every coiner of rebarbative language
is an Adorno.

The risks of specialized jargons for the humanities, inside
and outside the university, are obvious: they simply substitute
one prepackaged idiom for another. Why not assume instead
that the role of the humanistic exposition is to make the
demystifications and questionings that are so central to our
enterprise as transparent and as efficient as possible? Why turn
"bad writing" into an issue at all, except as a way of falling
into the trap of focusing uselessly on how something is said
rather than the more important issue of what is said? There
are too many available models of intelligible language all
around us whose basic graspability and efficiency goes the
whole range from difficult to comparatively simple, between

the language of, say, Henry James and that of W. E. B. DuBois. There is no need to employ preposterously outré and repellent idioms as a way of showing independence and originality. Humanism should be a form of disclosure, not of secrecy or religious illumination. Expertise as a distancing device has gotten out of control, especially in some academic forms of expression, to the extent that they have become antidemocratic and even anti-intellectual. At the heart of what I have been calling the movement of resistance in humanism—the first part of this being reception and reading—is critique, and critique is always restlessly self-clarifying in search of freedom, enlightenment, more agency, and certainly not their opposites.

None of this can be done easily. In the first place, the prepackaged information that dominates our patterns of thought (the media, advertising, official declarations, and ideological political argument designed to persuade or to lull into submission, not to stimulate thought and engage the intellect) tends to fit into short, telegraphic forms. CNN and the *New York Times* present information in headlines or sound bites, which are often followed by slightly longer periods of information whose stated purpose is to tell us what is happening "in reality." All the choices, exclusions, and emphases—to say nothing of the history of the subject at hand—are invisible, dismissed as irrelevant. What I have been calling humanistic resistance therefore needs to occur in longer forms, longer essays, longer periods of reflection, so that the early history of Saddam Hussein's government (always referred to deliberately as his "regime"), for example, can emerge in all its sordid detail, detail which includes an extensive pattern of direct U.S. support for him. Somebody needs to be able to present that as a way of guiding us as we go triumphantly from war to "reconstruction," with most Americans in the dark about Iraq itself, its history, its institutions, as well as our extensive dealings with it over the decades. None of this can be done in the form of short bursts of information concerning the "axis of evil" or stating that "Iraq possesses weapons of mass destruction and is a direct threat to the United States and our way of life," phrases that need laborious dismantling, unpacking, documentation, and refutation or confirmation. These are matters of the gravest importance for American humanists, who are citizens of the world's only superpower and whose acquiescence (or silence) are required for decisions of the greatest importance to us as informed citizens. Therefore humanistic reflection must literally break the hold on us of the short, headline, sound-bite format and try to induce instead a longer, more deliberate process of reflection, research, and inquiring argument that really looks at the case(s) in point.

A great deal more might be said about the question of language, but I want to press on to other concerns. There is no doubt, first of all, that whatever reading one does is situated in a particular time and place, just as the writing one encounters in the course of humanistic study is located in a series of frameworks derived from tradition, the transmission and variation of texts, and accumulated readings and interpretations. And just as important are the social contests that, generally, I shall describe as those between the aesthetic and historical domains. At the risk of simplifying, it can be said that two situations are in play: that of the humanistic reader in the present and that of the text in its framework. Each requires careful analysis, each inhabits both a local and a wider historical framework, and each must solicit relentless questioning by the humanist. The literary text derives, true enough, from the assumed privacy and solitude of the individual writer, but the tension between that privileged location and the social location of the writer is ever present, whether the writer is a historian like Henry Adams, a relatively isolated poet like Emily

Dickinson, or a renowned man of letters like Henry James. There is no way at all of focusing on either the original privacy or the public place of the writer without examining how each of them comes to us, whether by curricular canon, intellectual or critical frameworks provided by a presiding authority (such as that exercised by Perry Miller at one time), or a massive range of debate as to whose tradition this is, for what purpose, and so on. Immediately then, the constitution of tradition and the useable past comes up, and that in turn leads us inevitably to identity and the national state. A number of useful analyses both here and in England by Stuart Hall and Raymond Williams have discussed this matter: the enveloping national story with its carefully devised beginnings, middles, ends, its periods, moments of glory, defeat, triumph, and so on.

What I am trying to describe then is the created national horizon, in which humanistic study, with all its inner movements, disputed readings, contentious as well as cerebral ratiocinations, occurs. Now I want to caution against going from the private *ijtihad*, or close reading, to the wide horizon too quickly, too abruptly and unreflectively. But there can be no doubt that for me humanism as a worldly practice can move beyond and inhabit more than just the original privacy of the writer or the relatively private space of the classroom or inner sanctum, both of which are inevitably necessary to what we want to do as humanists. Education involves widening circles of awareness, each of which is distinct analytically while being connected to the others by virtue of worldly reality. A reader is in a place, in a school or university, in a work place, or in a specific country at a particular time, situation, and so forth. But these are not passive frameworks. In the process of widening the humanistic horizon, its achievements of insight and understanding, the framework must be actively understood, constructed, and interpreted. And this is what resistance is: the

ability to differentiate between what is directly given and what
may be withheld, whether because one's own circumstances as
a humanistic specialist may confine one to a limited space
beyond which one can't venture or because one is indoctri-
nated to recognize only what one has been educated to see or
because only policy experts are presumed to be entitled to
speak about the economy, health services, or foreign and military policies, issues of urgent concern to the humanist as a citizen. Does one accept the prevailing horizons and confine-
ments, or does one try as a humanist to challenge them?

This, I believe, is where the relevance of humanism to
contemporary America and the world of which it is a part has
to be addressed and understood if it is to make any sense
beyond teaching our students and fellow citizens how to read
well. This is an estimable task in itself, of course, but one that
by its own inventive energies also necessarily takes one further and further from even the most highly cherished inward
reception. Yes, we need to keep coming back to the words and
structures in the books we read, but, just as these words were
themselves taken by the poet from the world and evoked
from out of silence in the forceful ways without which no
creation is possible, readers must also extend their readings
out into the various worlds each one of us resides in. It is
especially appropriate for the contemporary humanist to cul-
tivate that sense of multiple worlds and complex interacting
traditions, that inevitable combination I've mentioned of
belonging and detachment, reception and resistance. The task
of the humanist is not just to occupy a position or place, nor
simply to belong somewhere, but rather to be both insider
and outsider to the circulating ideas and values that are at
issue in our society or someone else's society or the society of
the other. In this connection, it is invigorating to recall (as I
have in other places) Isaac Deutscher's insufficiently known
book of essays, *The Non-Jewish Jew*, for an account of how

great Jewish thinkers—Spinoza, chief among them, as well as Freud, Heine, and Deutscher himself—were in, and at the same time renounced, their tradition, preserving the original tie by submitting it to the corrosive questioning that took them well beyond it, sometimes banishing them from community in the process. Not many of us can or would want to aspire to such a dialectically fraught, so sensitively located a class of individuals, but it is illuminating to see in such a destiny the crystallized role of the American humanist, the nonhumanist humanist as it were.

In other words, if I were forced to choose for myself as humanist the role either of patriotically "affirming" our country as Richard Rorty has recently enunciated it (his word is "achieving," not affirming, but it amounts in the end to the same thing) or nonpatriotically questioning it, I would undoubtedly choose the role of questioner. Humanism, as Blackmur said of modernism in another connection, is a technique of trouble, and it must stay that way now at a time when the national and international horizon is undergoing massive transformations and reconfigurations. The task is constitutively an unending one, and it should not aspire to conclusion of the sort that has the corollary and, in my estimate deleterious, effect of securing one an identity to be fought over, defended, and argued, while a great deal about our world that is interesting and worth venturing into simply gets left aside. In the post–Cold War world, the politics of identity and partition (I speak only of aggressive identity politics, not the defense of identity when threatened by extinction, as in the Palestinian case) have brought more trouble and suffering than they are worth, nowhere more than when they are associated with precisely those things, such as the humanities, traditions, art, and values, that identity allegedly defends and safeguards, constituting in the process territories and selves that seem to require killing rather than living. There's been altogether too much of this in the United States since 9/11, with the result that meditative and nondogmatic examination of "our" role and traditions always seems to end up reinforcing the war against the whole world that the United States seems to be conducting.

What then can be more fitting for the humanist in the United States than to accept responsibility for maintaining rather than resolving the tension between the aesthetic and the national, using the former to challenge, reexamine and resist the latter in those slow but rational modes of reception and understanding which is the humanist's way. As for making those connections that allow us to see part and whole, that is the main thing: what to connect with, how, and how not?

It is necessary to discuss the agonistic moral universe embodied in a drama or novel and see in that aesthetic experience a searing incarnation of conflict and choice. But it is, I think, an abrogation of that reading to blind oneself to the similar drama in the battle all around us for justice, emancipation, and the diminishment of human suffering. Economics, for example, is misapprehended as the province only of the financial celebrities, CEOs and experts who gather annually at Davos (even there, however, one suspects that some turbulence is occurring), while the absolutely fundamental work of economists like Joseph Stieglitz and Amartya Sen on entitlement, distribution, poverty, famines, equity, and freedom has furnished a massive challenge to the market economics that rule nearly everywhere. I mention these two Nobel laureates as an instructive example of what, on all sides of the humanities, is occurring intellectually by way of movement in, reconfiguration of, and resistance to the overmastering paradigm of globalization and the false dichotomies offered, for instance, in the vulgarizing placations of Thomas Friedman in *The Lexus and the Olive Tree* or Benjamin Barber's *Jihad Versus McWorld*. What took place in November

1999 in Seattle or as a result of the health-care system insur-
gencies that disrupt hospitals when the corporate inequities
of HMOs become too much even for physicians, to say nothing of those millions of uninsured patients who have no care
at all—these are matters that are part of the humanistic horizon that our often quietistic disciplines have taught us not to
meddle with, but which need examination and resistance in
some of the deliberate ways I have been suggesting, albeit
briefly and only suggestively. And of course since 9/11 we
need even more care and skepticism in the bellicose
"defense" of our values than that which disaffected and perhaps even intimidated former dissenting intellectuals have
been urging on the country at large.

America's place in the world of nations and cultures,
when, as the last superpower, our foreign policy—based on
the projection and deployment of vast military, political, and
economic resources—has amounted to a new variety of
mostly unchallenged interventionism, has been a very significant aspect of America for humanists. To be a humanist here
and now in the United States is not the same thing as being
one in Brazil, India, or South Africa, and not even like being
one in a major European country. Who is "us" when the
nightly news commentator asks politely of the secretary of
state whether "our" sanctions against Saddam Hussein are
worth it, when literally millions of innocent civilians, not
members of that dreadful "regime," are being killed, maimed,
starved, and bombed so that we can make our power felt? Or
when a news reader asks the current secretary whether, in our
rage to prosecute Iraq for weapons of mass destruction
(which have not turned up anyway), "we" are going to apply
the same standard and ask Israel about its weapons, and
receives no answer at all.

The deployment of such pronouns as "we" and "us" are
also the stuff of lyrics and odes and dirges and tragedies, and

so it becomes necessary from the training we have had to raise the questions of responsibility and values, of pride and extraordinary arrogance, of an amazing moral blindness. Who is the "we" who bombs civilians or who shrugs off the looting and pillaging of Iraq's astonishing heritage with phrases like "stuff happens" or "freedom is untidy"? One ought to be able to say somewhere and at some length, I am not this "we" and what "you" do, you do not in my name.

Humanism is about reading, it is about perspective, and, in our work as humanists, it is about transitions from one realm, one area of human experience to another. It is also about the practice of identities other than those given by the flag or the national war of the moment. That deployment of an alternative identity is what we do when we read and when we connect parts of the text to others parts and when we go on to expand the area of attention to include widening circles of pertinence. Everything I have said about the humanities and humanism is based upon a stubborn conviction that must, that can only begin in the individual particular, without which there can be no real literature, no utterance worth making and cherishing, no human history and agency fit to protect and encourage. But one can be a nominalist and a realist and also remark on the leap to mobilized collective selves—without careful transition or deliberate reflection or with only unmediated assertion—that prove to be more destructive than anything they are supposedly defending. Those transitionless leaps are the ones to be looked at very hard and very severely. They lead to what Lukacs used to call totalities, unknowable existentially but powerfully mobilizing. They possess great force exactly because they are corporate and can stand in unjustifiably for action that is supposed to be careful, measured, and humane. "Our view," said Mrs. Albright, "is that these sanctions are worth it," "it" being the killing and destruction of numberless civilians genocidally dispatched by a phrase. The only word to break up the leap to such corporate banditry is the word "humane," and humanists without an exfoliating, elaborating, demystifying general humaneness are, as the phrase has it, sounding brass and tinkling cymbals. Naturally this gets us to the question of citizenship as well, but that is as it should be.

When humanists are enjoined or scolded to get back to their texts and leave the world to those whose job is to run it, it is salutary, indeed urgent, to be reminded that our age and our country symbolize not just what has been settled and permanently resides here, but always and constantly the undocumented turbulence of unsettled and unhoused exiles, immigrants, itinerant or captive populations for whom no document, no adequate expression yet exists sufficient to take account of what they go through. And in its profoundly unsettled energy, this country deserves the kind of widening awareness beyond academic specialization that a whole range of younger humanists have signaled as cosmopolitan, worldly, mobile.

Ironic, in this period of extremes, that even though this is the greatest age of documentary expansion and rapid, if flattening and one-dimensional, communication in history, it is also the one in which, I believe, more experience is being lost by marginalization and incorporation and homogenizing word processing than ever before, the experience of the undocumented peoples that are described so cavalierly now by our roving imperial reporters as residing at the ends of the earth. Humanism, I strongly believe, must excavate the silences, the world of memory, of itinerant, barely surviving groups, the places of exclusion and invisibility, the kind of testimony that doesn't make it onto the reports but which more and more is about whether an overexploited environment, sustainable small economies and small nations, and marginalized peoples outside as well as inside the maw of the metropolitan center can sur-

vive the grinding down and flattening out and displacement
that are such prominent features of globalization.

I should like to conclude with a thought that has been the
paramount feature of my always changing and, I'd like to think,
receptive and resistant practice as a humanist in the United
States: for that is the way I conceive of the area of concern for
humanistic attention, in spatial and geographical, rather than
exclusively in temporal, terms. The movements of our time and
of our country are movements in and out of territory: to be
moved in and off it, to try to stay, to try to establish new settle-
ments, and on and on in an implacable dynamic of place and
displacement that, in this endlessly mobile country of ours,
where the location of the frontier both metaphorical and real
appears never to be settled, is still very much the issue.

This moment seems to me the central fact of human history, perhaps because our own experiences as migrants, pil-
grims, and castaways in Eric Hobsbawm's short "century of
extremes," which has just ended, have colored our view of the
past so decisively, so politically and existentially. Often, as
Bourdieu writes, sites or places—be it a problem suburb or
ghetto or Chechnya, Kosovo, Iraq, or Africa—are phantasms,
which feed on emotional experiences stimulated by more or
less uncontrolled words and images, such as those conveyed
in the tabloids and by political propaganda or rumor. But to
break with accepted ideas and ordinary discourse (which on
one very profound level is what humanist reading is all
about), it is not enough, as we would sometimes like to think,
to "go see" what it's all about. In effect, the empiricist illusion
(which is so much the norm in contemporary media cover-
age of the world) is doubtless never so strong, as in cases like
this, where direct confrontation with reality entails some difficulty, even risk, and for that reason deserves some credit. Yet
there are compelling reasons to believe that the essential principle of what is lived and *seen on the ground* is elsewhere.

More than ever, then, we have to practice a *para-doxal mode of thought* (*doxa:* common sense, received ideals) that, being equally skeptical of good sense and fine sentiments, risks appearing to right-minded people on the two sides either as a position inspired by the desire to "shock the bourgeois" or else as an intolerable indifference to the suffering of the most disadvantaged people in our society. The suggestion is the late Pierre Bourdieu's, but it is useful for the American humanist too. "One can break with misleading appearances and with the errors inscribed in substantialist [that is, unmediated and without the modulated transitions I spoke about earlier] thought about place only through a rigorous analysis of the relations between the structures of social space and those of physical space" (123).

Humanism, I think, is the means, perhaps the consciousness we have for providing that kind of finally antinomian or oppositional analysis between the space of words and their various origins and deployments in physical and social place, from text to actualized site of either appropriation or resistance, to transmission, to reading and interpretation, from private to public, from silence to explication and utterance, and back again, as we encounter our own silence and mortality—all of it occurring in the world, on the ground of daily life and history and hopes, and the search for knowledge and justice, and then perhaps also for liberation.

References

Barber, Benjamin. Jihad Versus McWorld: *How Globalism and Tribalism Are Reshaping the World*. New York: Ballantine, 1996.

Bourdieu, Pierre. *The Weight of the World: Social Suffering in Contemporary Society*. Cambridge: Polity Press, 1999.

Deutscher, Isaac. *The Non-Jewish Jew*. Ed. and intro. Tamara Deutscher. London and New York: Oxford University Press, 1968.

Emerson, Ralph Waldo. *Essays: First and Second Series*. New York: Vintage Books, 1990.

Forster, E. M. *Howard's End*. New York: Penguin Classics, 1988.

Harlan, David Craig. *The Degradation of American History*. Chicago: University of Chicago Press, 1997.

Hobsbawm, Eric J. *The Age of Extremes, 1914–91*. London: Michael Joseph, 1994.

Poirier, Richard. *The Renewal of Literature: Emersonian Reflections*. New York: Random House, 1987.

Rorty, Richard. *Achieving Our Country: Leftist Thought in Twentieth-Century America*. Cambridge, Mass.: Harvard University Press, 1998.

Scarry, Elaine. *On Beauty and Being Just*. Princeton, N.J.: Princeton University Press, 1999.

Spitzer, Leo. "Linguistics and Literary History." In *Linguistics and Literary History: Essays in Stylistics*, by Leo Spitzer, 1–39. Princeton, N.J.: Princeton University Press, 1948.

4

INTRODUCTION TO ERICH AUERBACH'S
MIMESIS

Preface

AS THIS CHAPTER IS A PART OF THIS SERIES OF REFLECTIONS on humanism, I'd like to explain why it is about only one work and only one author, who doesn't happen to have been American in the literal sense. Rather than continuing my remarks on humanism, I thought it would be best if I could concretely illustrate my arguments by looking at a work that has had a lifelong importance to me and, despite the fact that it appeared fifty years ago, one that still seems to embody the best in humanistic work that I know. Auerbach's *Mimesis* was written in German in Istanbul, during World War II, but it appeared in English in the United States in 1953. Auerbach came to America after the war and remained here as a professor at Yale until his death in 1957, an American humanist by adoption, as it were. There is an extraordinarily gripping drama to the author and book I am going to discuss, which I hope I can communicate to the reader of this set of lectures. *Mimesis* is the greatest and most influential literary humanistic work of the past half century. It engages a great deal of what I have been talking about in the three chapters that precede it, and it may be read as an example of humanistic practice of its highest.

Mimesis

> Human beings are not born once and for all on the day their mothers give birth to them, but that life obliges them to give birth to themselves.

—Gabriel García Márquez

The influence and enduring reputation of books of criticism are (for the critics who write them and hope to be read for more than one season) dispiritingly short. Since World War II, the sheer volume of books appearing in English has risen to a huge amount, thus further ensuring if not ephemerality, then a relatively short life and hardly any influence at all. Books of criticism have usually come in waves associated with academic trends, most of which are quickly replaced by successive shifts in taste, fashion, or genuine intellectual discovery. Thus only a small number of books seem perennially present and, by comparison with the vast majority of their counterparts, have an amazing staying power. Certainly this is true most obviously, in my opinion, of Erich Auerbach's magisterial *Mimesis: The Representation of Reality in Western Literature*, published by Princeton University Press exactly fifty years ago in a satisfyingly readable English translation by Willard R. Trask.

As one can immediately judge by its subtitle, Auerbach's book is by far the largest in scope and ambition of any of the others. Its range covers literary masterpieces from Homer and the Old Testament right through to Virginia Woolf and Marcel Proust, although, as Auerbach says apologetically at the end of the book, for reasons of space he had to leave out a great deal of medieval literature as well as some crucial modern writers like Pascal and Baudelaire. He was to treat the former in his last, posthumously published book, *Literary Language and Its Public in Late Latin Antiquity and in the Middle Ages*, and the latter in various journals and a collection of his essays, *Scenes From the Drama of European Literature.* In all these works, Auerbach preserves the same essayistic style of criticism, beginning each chapter with a long quotation from a specific work cited in the original language, followed immediately by a serviceable translation (German in the original *Mimesis*, first published in Bern in 1946, English in most of his subsequent work), out of which a detailed *explication de texte* unfolds at a leisurely and ruminative pace; this in turn develops into a set of memorable comments about the relationship between the rhetorical style of the passage and its sociopolitical context, a feat that Auerbach manages with a minimum of fuss and with virtually no learned references. He explains in the concluding chapter of *Mimesis* that even had he wanted to, he couldn't make use of the available scholarly resources, first of all because he was in wartime Istanbul when the book was written and no Western research libraries were accessible for him to consult, second because had he been able to use references from the extremely voluminous secondary literature, the material would have swamped him and he would never have written the book. Thus, along with the primary texts which he had with him, Auerbach relied mainly on memory and what seems like an infallible interpretive skill for elucidating relationships between books and the world they belonged to.

Even in English translation, the hallmark of Auerbach's style is a tone of unruffled and at times even lofty and supreme calm, conveying a combination of quiet erudition allied with an overridingly patient and loving confidence in his mission as scholar and philologist. But who was he, and what sort of

background and training did he have that enabled him to produce such work of truly outstanding influence and longevity?
By the time *Mimesis* appeared in English he was already sixty-
one, the son of a German Jewish family residing in Berlin, the
city where he was born in 1892. By all accounts he received a
classic Prussian education, graduating from that city's
renowned Französisches Gymnasium, or elite high school,
where the German and the Franco-Latin traditions were
brought together in a very special way. He received a doctorate in law from Heidelberg in 1913 and then served in the
German army during World War I, after which he abandoned
law and took a doctorate in Romance languages at the University of Greifswald. Geoffrey Green, author of an important
book on Auerbach, has speculated that "the violence and horrors" of the war experience may have caused the change in
career from legal to literary pursuits, from "the vast, stolid legal
institutions of society . . . to [an investigation of] the distant,
shifting patterns of philological studies" (Green, 20–21).

Between 1923 and 1929, Auerbach held a position at
Berlin's Prussian State Library. It was then that he strength-
ened his grasp of the philological vocation and produced two
major pieces of work, a German translation of Giambattista
Vico's *New Science* and a seminal monograph on Dante entitled *Dante als Dichter der Irdischen Welt* (when the book
appeared in English in 1961 as, *Dante, Poet of the Secular World*,
the crucial word *Irdischen,* or earthly, was only partially rendered by the considerably less concrete "secular.") Auerbach's
lifelong preoccupation with these two Italian authors under-
scores the specific and concrete character of his attention, so
unlike that of contemporary critics who prefer what is
implicit to what the text actually says.

In the first place, Auerbach's thought is anchored in the tradition of Romance philology, the study of those literatures
deriving from Latin but, interestingly, ideologically unintelli-

gible without the Christian doctrine of Incarnation (and hence the Roman Church) as well as its secular underpinning in the Holy Roman Empire. An additional factor was the development out of Latin of the various demotic languages, from Provençal to French, Italian, Spanish, and so on. Far from being the dry-as-dust academic study of word origins, philology, for Auerbach and eminent contemporaries of his like Karl Vossler, Leo Spitzer, and Ernst Robert Curtius, was in effect an immersion in all the available written documents in one or several Romance languages, from numismatics to epigraphy, from stylistics to archival research, from rhetoric and law to an all-embracing working idea of literature that included chronicles, epics, sermons, drama, stories, and essays. Inherently comparative, Romance philology in the early twentieth century derived its main procedural ideas from a principally German tradition of interpretation that begins with the Homeric criticism of Friederich August Wolf (1759–1824), continues through Herman Schleiermacher's biblical criticism, includes some of the most important works of Nietzsche (who was a classical philologist by profession) and culminated in the often laboriously articulated philosophy of Wilhelm Dilthey.

Dilthey argued that the world of written texts (of which the aesthetic masterwork was the central pillar) belonged to the realm of lived experience (*erlebnis*), which the interpreter attempted to recover through a combination of erudition and a subjective intuition (*einfülung*) of what the inner spirit (*Geist*) of the work was. Dilthey's ideas about knowledge rest on an initial distinction between the world of nature (and natural sciences) and the world of spiritual objects, the basis of whose knowledge he classified as a mixture of objective and subjective elements, *Geisteswissenschaft*, or knowledge of the products of mind or spirit. Whereas there is no real English or American equivalent for it (although the study of culture is a rough approximation), it is a recognized academic sphere in the

German-speaking countries. In his later addendum, *The Epilo-gomena* (1953) to *Mimesis*, Auerbach says explicitly that his work "arose from the themes and methods of German intellectual history and philology; it would be conceivable in no other tradition than in that of German romanticism and Hegel."

While it is possible to appreciate Auerbach's *Mimesis* for its fine, absorbing explication of individual, sometimes obscure texts, one needs to disentangle its various antecedents and components, many of which are quite unfamiliar to modern readers but which Auerbach sometimes refers to in passing and always takes for granted in the course of his book. Auerbach's lifelong interest in the eighteenth-century Neopolitan professor of Latin eloquence and jurisprudence Giambattista Vico is absolutely central to his work as critic and philologist. In the posthumously published 1745 third edition of his magnum opus *La scienza nuova*, Vico formulated a revolutionary discovery of astonishing power and brilliance. Quite on his own, and as a reaction to Cartesian abstractions about ahistorical and contextless clear and distinct ideas, Vico argues that human beings are historical creatures in that they make history, or what he called "the world of the nations.

Understanding or interpreting history is therefore possible only because "men made it," since we can only know what we have made (just as only God knows nature because he made it). Knowledge of the past that comes to us in textual form, Vico says, can only be properly understood from the point of view of the maker of that past which, in the case of ancient writers such as Homer, is primitive, barbaric, poetic. In Vico's private lexicon, the word "poetic" means primitive and barbaric, vivid and truly inventive, because early human beings could not think rationally but could fantasize with reckless attractive ease. Examining the Homeric epics from the perspective of when and by whom they were composed, Vico refutes generations of interpreters who had assumed that because Homer was revered for his great epics he must also have been a wise sage like Plato, Socrates, or Bacon. Instead, Vico demonstrates that in its wildness and willfulness Homer's mind was poetic, and his poetry was barbaric not wise or philosophic, that is, full of illogical fantasy, gods who were anything but godlike, men like Achilles and Patrocles who were most uncourtly and extremely petulant.

This primitive mentality was Vico's great discovery, and its influence on European romanticism and its cult of the imagination was profound. Vico also formulated a theory of historical coherence that showed how each period shared in its language, art, metaphysics, logic, science, law, and religion features that were common and appropriate to their appearance: primitive times produce primitive knowledge that was a projection of the barbaric mind—fantastic images of gods based on fear, guilt, and terror—and this in turn gave rise to institutions such as marriage and the burial of the dead, which preserve the human race and give it a sustained history. The poetic age of giants and barbarians is succeeded by the age of heroes, and that slowly evolves into the age of men. Thus human history and society are created, a laborious process of unfolding, development, contradiction, and, most interestingly, representation. Each age has its own method, or optic, for seeing and then articulating reality: thus Plato develops his thought *after* (and not during) the period of violently concrete poetic images through which Homer spoke. The age of poetry gave way to a time when a greater degree of abstraction and rational discursivity became dominant.

All these developments occur as a cycle that goes from primitive to advanced and degenerate epochs, then back to primitive, Vico says, according to the modifications of the human mind, which makes and then can reexamine its own history from the point of view of the maker. That is the main methodological point for Vico as well as Auerbach. In order

to be able to understand a humanistic text, one must try to
do so as if one is the author of that text, living the author's
reality, undergoing the kind of life experiences intrinsic to
the author's life, and so forth, all by that combination of erudition and sympathy that is the hallmark of philological
hermeneutics. Thus the line between actual events and the
modifications of one's own reflective mind is blurred in Vico,
as it is in the numerous authors who were influenced by him,
such as James Joyce. But this perhaps tragic shortcoming of
human knowledge and history is one of the unresolved contradictions pertaining to humanism itself, in which the role of
thought in reconstructing the past can neither be excluded
nor squared with what is "real." Hence Auerbach's subtitle,
"the representation of reality" for *Mimesis* and the vacillations
in the book between learning and personal insight.

By the early part of the nineteenth century, Vico's work had
become tremendously influential to European historians,
poets, novelists, and philologists, from Michelet and Coleridge
to Marx and Joyce. Auerbach's fascination with Vico's historicism (sometimes called historism) underwrote his hermeneutical philology and allowed him to read texts such as those by
Augustine or Dante from the point of view of the author,
whose relationship to his age was an organic and integral one,
a kind of self-making within the context of the specific
dynamics of society at a very precise moment in its development. Moreover, the relationship between the reader–critic
and the text is transformed, from a one-way interrogation of
the historical text by an altogether alien mind at a much later
time, into a sympathetic dialogue of two spirits across ages and
cultures who are able to communicate with each other as
friendly, respectful imtelligences trying to understand each
other from the other's perspective.

Now it is quite obvious that such an approach requires a
great deal of erudition, although it is also clear that for the Ger-

man Romance philologists of the early twentieth century, with their formidable training in languages, history, literature, law, theology, and general culture, mere erudition was not enough. Obviously, one couldn't do the basic reading if one hadn't mastered Latin, Greek, Hebrew, Provençal, Italian, French, and Spanish, in addition to German and English, their traditions, main canonical authors, the politics, institutions, and cultures of the time, as well as all of their interconnected arts. A philologist's training had to take many years, although in Auerbach's case he gives one the attractive impression that he was in no hurry to get on with it. He landed his first academic teaching job with a chair at the University of Marburg in 1929; this was the result of his Dante book, which in many ways, I think, is his most exciting and intense work. But in addition to learning and study, the heart of the hermeneutical enterprise was to develop over the years a very particular kind of sympathy toward texts from different periods and different cultures. For a German whose specialty was Romance literature, this sympathy took on an almost ideological cast, given that there had been a long period of historical enmity between Prussia and France, the most powerful and competitive of its neighbors and antagonists. As a specialist in Romance languages, the German scholar had a choice either to enlist on behalf of Prussian nationalism (as Auerbach did as a soldier during the First World War) and study "the enemy" with skill and insight as a part of the continuing war effort, or, as was the case with Auerbach and his peers, to overcome bellicosity and what we now call "the clash of civilizations" with a welcoming, hospitable attitude of humanistic knowledge designed to realign warring cultures in a relationship of mutuality and reciprocity.

The other part of the German Romance philologist's commitment to French, Italian, and Spanish generally and French in particular is specifically literary. The historical trajectory which is the spine of *Mimesis* is the passage from the separation of styles in classical antiquity to their mingling in the New Testament, their first great climax in Dante's *Divine Comedy*, and their ultimate apotheosis in the French realistic authors of the nineteenth century, Stendhal, Balzac, Flaubert, and then Proust. The representation of reality is Auerbach's theme, so he had to make a judgment as to where and in what literature it was most ably represented. In the *Epilegomenon* he explains that "in most periods the Romance literatures are more representative of Europe than are, for example, the German. In the twelfth and thirteenth centuries France unquestionably took the leading role; in the fourteenth and fifteenth centuries Italy took it over; it fell again to France in the seventeenth, remained there also during the greater part of the eighteenth, partly still in the nineteenth, and precisely for the origin and development of modern realism (just as for painting)" (570). I think Auerbach scants the substantial English contribution in all this, perhaps a blind spot in his vision. Auerbach goes on to affirm that these judgments derive not from aversion to German culture but rather from a sense of regret that German literature "expressed . . . certain limitations of outlook in . . . the nineteenth century" (571). As we shall soon see, he doesn't specify what those were, as he had done in the body of *Mimesis*, but adds that "for pleasure and relaxation" he still prefers reading Goethe, Stifter, and Keller over the French authors he studies, going as far once as saying after a remarkable analysis of Baudelaire that he didn't like him at all (571).

For English readers today who associate Germany principally with horrendous crimes against humanity and National Socialism (which Auerbach circumspectly alludes to several times in *Mimesis*), the tradition of hermeneutical philology embodied by Auerbach as a Romance specialist identifies just as authentic an aspect of classical German culture, its methodological generosity and, in what might seem like a contradiction, its extraordinary attention to the minute, local detail of

other cultures and languages. The great progenitor and clari-
fier of this extremely catholic, indeed almost altruistic attitude
is Goethe, who in the decade after 1810 became fascinated
with Islam generally and Persian poetry in particular. This was
the period when he composed his finest and most intimate
love poetry, the *West-Oestlicher Diwan* (West-eastern divan;
1819), finding in the work of the great Persian poet Hafiz and
in the verses of the Koran not only a new lyric inspiration
allowing him to express a reawakened sense of physical love
but, as he said in a letter to his good friend Zelter, a discovery
of how, in the absolute submission to God, he felt himself to
be oscillating between two worlds, his own and that of the
Muslim believer who was miles, even worlds away from European Weimar. During the 1820s, those earlier thoughts carried
him toward a conviction that national literatures had been
superseded by what he called *Weltliteratur*, or world literature,
a universalist conception of all the literatures of the world seen
together as forming a majestic symphonic whole.

For many modern scholars—including myself—Goethe's
grandly utopian vision is considered to be the foundation of
what was to become the field of comparative literature, whose
underlying and perhaps unrealizable rationale was this vast
synthesis of the world's literary production transcending borders and languages, but not in any way effacing the individuality and historical concreteness of its constituent parts. In
1951, Auerbach wrote an autumnal, reflective essay entitled
"Philology and *Weltliteratur*" in a somewhat pessimistic tone
because he felt that with the greater specialization of knowledge and expertise after the Second World War, the dissolution
of the educational and professional institutions in which he
had been trained, and the emergence of "new" non-European
literatures and languages, the Goethean ideal might have
become invalid or untenable. But for most of his working life
as a Romance philologist, he was a man with a mission, a

European (and Euroecentric) mission it is true, but something he deeply believed in for its emphasis on the unity of human history, the possibility it granted of understanding inimical and perhaps even hostile Others despite the bellicosity of modern cultures and nationalisms, and the optimism with which one could enter into the inner life of a distant author or historical epoch even with a healthy awareness of one's limitations of perspective and insufficiency of knowledge.

Such noble intentions were insufficient, however, to save his career after 1933. In 1935, he was forced to quit his position in Marburg, a victim of Nazi racial laws and an atmosphere of increasingly jingoistic mass culture presided over by intolerance and hatred. A few months later he was offered a position teaching Romance literatures at the Istanbul State University, where some years before Leo Spitzer had also taught. It was while he was in Istanbul, Auerbach tells us in the concluding pages of *Mimesis*, that he wrote and finished the book, which then appeared in Switzerland one year after the war's end. And even though the book is in many ways a calm affirmation of the unity and dignity of European literature in all its multiplicity and dynamism, it is also a book of countercurrents, ironies, and even contradictions that need to be taken into account for it to be read and understood properly. This rigorously fastidious attention to particulars, to details, to individuality is why *Mimesis* is not principally a book that provides readers with useable concepts, which, in the case of instances like the Renaissance, baroque, romantic, or other genres, are not exact; they are unscientific, as well as finally unusable. "Our precision [as philologists]," he says,

> relates to the particular. The progress of the historical arts in the last two centuries consists above all, apart from the opening up of new material and in a great refinement of methods in individual research, in a perspectival formation of judgment, which

> makes it possible to accord the various epochs and cultures
> their own presuppositions and views, to strive to the utmost
> toward the discovery of those, and to dismiss as unhistorical and
> dilettantish every absolute assessment of the phenomena that is
> brought in from outside. (Auerbach, 15–16)

Thus for all its redoubtable learning and authority, *Mimesis* is also a personal book, disciplined, yes, but not autocratic and not pedantic. Consider first of all that even though *Mimesis* is the product of an extraordinarily thorough education and is steeped in an unparalleled inwardness and familiarity with European culture, it is an exile's book, written by a German cut off from his roots and his native environment. Auerbach seems not to have wavered, however, in his loyalty to his Prussian upbringing or his feeling that he always expected to return to Germany. "I am a Prussian and of the Jewish faith," he wrote of himself in 1921, and despite his later diasporic existence he did not seem to have doubted where he really belonged. American friends and colleagues report that until his final illness and death in 1957, he was looking for some way to return to Germany. Nevertheless, after all those years in Istanbul he undertook a new postwar career in the United States, spending time at the Princeton Institute for Advanced Study and as a professor at Pennsylvania State University before he went to Yale as Sterling Professor of Romance Philology in 1956.

Auerbach's Jewishness is something one can only speculate about since, in his typically reticent way, he doesn't refer to it directly in *Mimesis*. One assumes, for instance, that the various intermittent comments throughout the book about mass modernity and its relationship with, among others, the disruptive power of the nineteenth-century French realistic writers (the Goncourts, Balzac, and Flaubert) as well as "the tremendous crisis" it caused, are meant movingly to suggest the menacing world and how that world affects the transformation of reality and consequently of style (the development of the *sermo humilis* due to the figure of Jesus). It is not hard to detect a combination of pride and distance as he describes the emergence of Christianity in the ancient world as the product of prodigious missionary work undertaken by the apostle Paul, a diaspora Jew converted to Christ. The parallel with his own situation as a non-Christian explaining Christianity's achievement is evident, but so too is the irony that in so doing he travels from his roots still further. Most of all, however, in Auerbach's searingly powerful and strangely intimate characterization of the great Christian Thomist poet Dante—who emerges from the pages of *Mimesis* as *the* seminal figure in Western literature—the reader is inevitably led to the paradox of a Prussian Jewish scholar in Turkish, Muslim, non-European exile handling (perhaps even juggling) a charged and in many ways irreconcilable set of antinomies that, though he appears to order them more benignly than their mutual antagonism suggests, never lose their opposition to one another. Auerbach is a firm believer in the dynamic transformations as well as the deep sedimentations of history: yes, Judaism made Christianity possible through Paul, but Judaism remained and it remains different from Christianity. So too, he says in a melancholy passage in *Mimesis*, will collective passions remain the same whether in Roman times or under National Socialism. What makes these meditations so poignant is an autumnal but unmistakably authentic sense of humanistic mission that is both tragic and hopeful. I shall return to these matters later.

I think it is quite proper to highlight some of the more personal aspects of *Mimesis* because in many ways it is and should be read as an unconventional book. Of course it has the manifest gravity of the Important Book, but, as I noted above, it is by no means a formulaic book, despite the relative simplicity of its main theses about literary style in Western literature. In classical literature, Auerbach says, high style was used for nobles and gods who could be treated tragically, low style was principally for comic and mundane subjects, perhaps even for idyllic ones, but the idea of everyday human or worldly life as something to be represented through a style proper to it is not generally available before Christianity. Tacitus, for example, is simply not interested in talking about or representing the everyday, excellent historian though he is. If we go back to Homer, as Auerbach does in the celebrated, and much anthologized first chapter of *Mimesis,* the style is paratactic, that is, it deals with reality as a line of "externalized, uniformly illuminated phenomena, at a definite time and in a definite place, connected together without lacunae in a perpetual foreground [which, technically speaking, is parataxis, words and phrases added on rather than subordinated to each other]; thoughts and feelings completely expressed; events taking place in leisurely fashion and with very little of suspense" (11). So as he analyzes the return to Ithaca by Odysseus, Auerbach notes how the author simply narrates his greeting and recognition by the old nurse Euryclea who knows him by the childhood scar he bears the moment she washes his feet: past and present are on an equal footing, there is no suspense, and one has the impression that nothing is held back, despite the inherent precariousness of the episode, what with Penelope's interloping suitors hanging about, waiting to kill her returning husband.

On the other hand, Auerbach's consideration of the Abraham and Isaac story in the Old Testament beautifully demonstrates how it

> is like a silent progress through the indeterminate and the contingent, a holding of the breath . . . the overwhelming suspense is present. . . . The personages speak in the Bible story too; but their speech does not serve, as does speech in Homer, to manifest, to externalize thoughts—on the contrary, it serves to indi-

cate thoughts which remain unexpressed . . . [there is an] exter-
nalization of only so much of the phenomena as is necessary for
the purpose of the narrative, all else left in obscurity; the decisive
points of the narrative alone are emphasized, what lies beneath
is nonexistent; time and place are undefined and call for interpretation; thoughts and feeling remain unexpressed, are only
suggested by silence and the fragmentary speeches; the whole is
permeated with the most unrelieved suspense and directed
toward a single goal (and to that extent far more of a unity),
remains mysterious and "fraught with background." (11–12)

Moreover, these contrasts can be seen in representations of
human beings, in Homer of heroes "who wake every morn-
ing as if it were the first day of their lives," whereas the Old
Testament figures, including God, are heavy with the impli-
cation of extending into the depths of time, space, and consciousness, hence of character, and therefore require a much
more concentrated, intense act of attention from the reader.

A great part of Auerbach's charm as a critic is that, far from
seeming heavy-handed and pedantic, he exudes a sense of
searching and discovery, the joys and uncertainties of which
he shares unassumingly with his reader. Nelson Lowry Jr., a
younger colleague of his at Yale, wrote aptly in a memorial
note of the self-instructing quality of Auerbach's work:

He was his own best teacher and learner. That process goes
on in one's head, and one can become publicly aware of it to
the extent of reproducing some of its primeval dramatic unfolding. The point is *how* you arrive, by what dangers, mistakes, for-
tuitous encounters, sleeps or slips of mind, by what insights
achieved through great expense of time and passion and to what
hard-won formulations in the face of history. . . . Auerbach had
the ability to start with a single text without being coy, to
expound it with a freshness that might pass for naiveté, to avoid
making mere thematic or arbitrary connections, and yet to
begin to weave ample fabrics from a single loom. (Lowry, 318)

As the 1953 *Epilegomenon* demonstrates, however, Auerbach was adamant (if not also fierce) in rebutting criticisms of his claims; there's a specially tart exchange with his polymathic Romance colleague Ernst Robert Curtius which shows the two formidable scholars slugging it out rather belligerently.

I think it's not an exaggeration to say that, like Vico, Auerbach was at bottom an autodidact, guided in his diverse explorations by a handful of deeply conceived and complex themes with which he wove his ample fabric, which wasn't seamless or effortlessly spun out. In *Mimesis,* he resolutely sticks to his practice of working from disconnected fragments; each of the book's chapters is marked not only by a new author who bears little overt relationship to earlier fragments, but also a new beginning in terms of the author's perspective and stylistic outlook, so to speak. The "representation" of reality is taken by Auerbach to mean an active dramatic presentation of how each author actually realizes, brings characters to life, clarifies his or her own world; this of course explains why in reading the book we are compelled by the sense of disclosure that Auerbach affords us as he in turn re-realizes and interprets and, in his unassuming way, even seems to be staging the transmutation of a coarse reality into language and new life.

One major theme turns up quickly in the first chapter: the notion of incarnation, a centrally Christian idea, of course, whose prehistory in Western literature Auerbach ingeniously locates in the contrast between Homer and the Old Testament. The difference between Homer's Odysseus and the Bible's Abraham is that the former is immediately present and requires no interpretation, no recourse either to allegory or complicated explanations. Diametrically opposed is the figure of Abraham, who incarnates "doctrine and promise" and is steeped in them. These are "inseparable from" him and "for that very reason are fraught with 'background' and [are] mysterious, containing a second, concealed meaning" (15). And this second meaning can only be recovered by a very particular act of interpretation, which, in the main piece of work Auerbach produced in Istanbul before he published *Mimesis* in 1946, he described as figural interpretation. (I refer here to Auerbach's long and rather technical essay "Figura," published in 1944 and now available in *Scenes From the Drama of European Literature*).

This is another instance where Auerbach seems to be negotiating between the Jewish and European (hence Christian) components of his identity. Basically, figural interpretation developed as early Christian thinkers such as Tertullian and Augustine felt impelled to reconcile the Old and New Testaments. Both parts of the Bible were the word of God, but how were they related, how could they be read, as it were, together, given the quite considerable difference between the old Judaic dispensation and the new message emanating from the Christian Incarnation?

The solution arrived at, according to Auerbach, is the notion that the Old Testament prophetically prefigures the New Testament, which in turn can be read as a figural and, he adds, carnal (hence incarnate, real, worldly) realization or interpretation of the Old Testatment. The first event or figure is "real and historical announcing something else that is also real and historical." At last we begin to see, like interpretation itself, how history doesn't only move forward but also backward, in each oscillation between eras managing to accomplish a greater realism, a more substantial "thickness" (to use a term from current anthropological description), a higher degree of truth.

In Christianity, the core doctrine is that of the mysterious Logos, the Word made flesh, God made into a man, and therefore literally, incarnated, but how much more fulfilling is the new idea that pre-Christian times can be read as a shadowy figure (*figura*) of what actually was to come? Auerbach quotes a sixth-century cleric as saying "that figure [a character or episode in the Old Testament that prophesies something comparable in the New Testament], without which not a letter of the Old Testament exists, now at length endures to better purpose in the New"; and from just about the same time [Auerbach continues] a passage in the writings of Bishop Avitus of Vienne . . . in which he speaks of the Last Judgment; just as God in killing the first-born in Egypt spared the houses daubed with blood, so may He recognize and spare the faithful by the sign of the Eucharist: *tu cognosce tuam salvanda in plebe figuram* ("recognize thine own figure in the people that are to be saved"). (46–47)

One last and quite difficult aspect of *figura* needs pointing out here. Auerbach contends that the very concept of *figura* also functions as a middle term between the literal-historical dimension and, for the Christian author, the world of truth, *veritas.* So rather than conveying only an inert meaning for an episode or character in the past, in its second and more interesting sense *figura* is the intellectual and spiritual energy that does the actual connecting between past and present, history and Christian truth, which is so essential to interpretation. "In this connection," Auerbach claims, "*figura* is roughly equivalent to *spiritus* or *intellectus spiritalis,* sometimes replaced by *figuralitus*" (47). Thus for all the complexity of his argument and the minuteness of the often arcane evidence he presents, Auerbach, I believe, is bringing us back to what is an essentially Christian doctrine for believers but also a crucial element of *human* intellectual power and will. In this he follows Vico, who looks at the whole of human history and says, "mind made all this," an affirmation that audaciously reaffirms, but also to some degree undercuts, the religious dimension that gives credit to the divine.

Auerbach's own vacillation between his extraordinarily erudite and sensitive care for the intricacies of Christian symbolism and doctrine and his resolute secularism (and perhaps also his own Jewish background), his unwavering focus on the earthly, the historical, the worldly, gives *Mimesis* a very fruitful kind of inner tension. Certainly it is the finest work we have that describes the millennial effects of Christianity on literary representation. But it also glorifies as much as it animates with singular force and individualistic genius, most overtly in the chapters on verbal virtuosity in Dante, Rabelais, and Shakespeare. As we shall see in a moment, their creativity vies with God's in setting the human in a timeless as well as temporal setting. Typically, however, Auerbach chooses to express such ideas as an integral part of his unfolding interpretive quest in the book: he therefore doesn't take time out to explain it methodologically but lets it emerge from the very history of the representation of reality as *it* begins to gather density and scope. Remember that as his point of departure for analysis (which in a later essay he referred to and discussed as the *Ansatzpunkt*), Auerbach always comes back to the text and to the stylistic means used by the author to represent reality. This excavation of semantic meaning is most virtuosically evident in the essay "Figura" and in such brilliant shorter studies as his fertile examination of single phrases like "*la cour et la ville*," which contain a whole library of meanings that illuminate seventeenth-century French society and culture.

Three seminal moments in the trajectory of *Mimesis* should now be identified in some detail. One is to be found in the book's second chapter, "Fortunata," whose starting point is a passage by the Roman author Petronius followed by another by Tacitus. Both men treat their subjects from a one-sided point of view, that of writers concerned with maintaining the rigid social order of high and low classes. The wealthy and the important personages get all the attention, while the commoners or vulgar people are relegated to unimportance and obscurity. After having illustrated the insufficiencies of this classical separation of styles into high and low, Auerbach develops a wonderful contrast with that agonizing nocturnal moment in the Gospel of St. Mark when, standing in the courtyard of the High Priest's palace peopled with servant girls and soldiers, Simon Peter denies his relationship to the imprisoned Jesus. One particularly eloquent passage from *Mimesis* deserves quotation:

> It is apparent at first glance that the rule of differentiated styles cannot possibly apply in this case. The incident, entirely realistic in regard to locale and *dramatis personae*—note particularly their low social station—is replete with problem and tragedy. Peter is no mere accessory figure serving as *illustratio*, like the soldiers Vibulenus and Percennius [in Tacitus], who are represented as mere scoundrels and swindlers. He is the image of man in the highest and deepest and most tragic sense. Of course this mingling of styles is not dictated by an artistic purpose. On the contrary, it was rooted from the beginning in the character of Jewish-Christian literature; it was graphically and harshly dramatized through God's incarnation in a human being of the humblest social station, through his existence on earth amid humble everyday people and conditions, and through his Passion which, judged by earthly standards, was ignominious; and it naturally came to have . . . a most decisive bearing upon man's conception of the tragic and the sublime. Peter, whose personal account may have been assumed to have been the basis of the story, was a fisherman from Galilee, of humblest background and humblest education. . . . From the humdrum existence of his daily life, Peter is called to the most tremendous role. Here, like everything else to do with Jesus' arrest, his appearance on the world stage—viewed in the world-historical continuity of the Roman Empire—is nothing but a provincial incident, an insignificant local occurrence, noted by none but those directly involved. Yet how tremendous it is, viewed in relation to the life a fisherman from the Sea of Galilee normally lives. (41–42)

Auerbach then goes on unhurriedly to detail the "pendulation" or swings in Peter's soul between sublimity and fear, faith and doubt, courage and defeat in order to show that those experiences are radically incompatible with "the sublime style of classical antique literature." This still leaves the question of why such a passage moves us, given that in classical literature it would appear only as farce or comedy. "Because it portrays something which neither the poets nor the historians of antiquity ever set out to portray: the birth of a spiritual movement in the depths of the common people, from within the occurrences of contemporary life, which thus assures an importance it could never have assumed in antique literature. What we witness is the awakening of 'a new heart and a new passion.' All this applies not only to Peter's denial but to every other occurrence which is related in the New Testament" (42–43). What Auerbach enables us to see here is a world which on the one hand is entirely real, average, identifiable as to place, time, and circumstances, but which on the other hand "is shaken in its very foundations, is transforming and renewing itself before our eyes" (43).

Christianity shatters the classical balance between high and low styles, just as Jesus' life destroys the separation between the sublime and the everyday. What is set in motion as a result is the search for a new literary pact between writer and reader, a new synthesis or mingling between style and interpretation that will be adequate to the disturbing volatility of worldly events in the much grander setting opened up by Christ's historical presence. To this end, St. Augustine's enormous accomplishment, linked as he was to the classical world by his education, was to be the first to realize that classical antiquity had been superseded by a different world requiring a new *sermo humilis*, "a low style such as would properly only be applicable to comedy, but which now reaches out far beyond its original domain, and encroaches upon the deepest and the highest, the sublime and the eternal" (72). The problem then becomes how to relate the discursive, sequential events of human history to each other within the new figural dispensation that has triumphed conclusively over its predecessor, and then to find a language adequate to such a task, once, after the fall of the Roman Empire, Latin was no longer the lingua franca of Europe.

Auerbach's choice of Dante to represent the second seminal moment in Western literary history is made to seem breathtakingly appropriate. Read slowly and reflectively, chapter 8 of *Mimesis*, "Farinata and Cavalcante" is one of the great moments in modern critical literature, a masterly, almost vertiginous embodiment of Auerbach's own ideas about Dante, that the *Divine Comedy* synthesized the timeless and the historical because of Dante's genius, and that his use of the demotic (or vulgar) Italian language in a sense enabled the creation of what we have come to call literature. I won't try to summarize Auerbach's analysis of a passage from canto 10 of the *Inferno*, in which Dante the pilgrim and his guide Virgil are accosted by two Florentines who knew Dante from Florence but who are now committed to the Inferno, and whose internecine squabbles between the city's Guelph and Ghibelline factions carry on into the afterworld: readers should experience this dazzling analysis for themselves. Auerbach notes that the seventy lines he focuses on are incredibly packed, containing no less than four separate scenes, as well as more varied material than any other so far discussed in *Mimesis*. What particularly compels the reader is that Dante's Italian in the poem is, as Auerbach puts it assertively, "a well-nigh incomprehensible miracle," used by the poet "to discover the world anew" (182–83).

There is first of all the language's combination of "sublimity and triviality which, measured by the standards of antiquity, is monstrous." Then there is its immense forcefulness, "its repulsive and often disgusting greatness," according to Goethe, whereby the poet uses the vernacular to represent "the antagonism of the two traditions . . . that of antiquity . . . and that of the Christian era . . . Dante's powerful tempera- ment, which is conscious of both because its aspiration toward the tradition of antiquity does not imply for it the possibility of abandoning the other; nowhere does mingling of styles come so close to violation of all style" (184–85). Then there is its abundance of material and styles, all of it treated in what Dante claimed was "the common everyday language of the people" (186), which allowed a realism that brought forth descriptions of the classical, the biblical, and the everyday worlds "not displayed in a single action, but instead an abun- dance of actions in the most diverse tonalities [which] follow one another in quick succession" (189). And finally, Dante manages to achieve through his style a combination of past, present, and future, since the two Florentine men who rise out of their flaming tombs to accost Dante so peremptorily are in fact dead but seem to live on somehow in what Hegel called a "changeless existence," remarkably devoid neither of history nor of memory and facticity. Having been judged for their sins and placed inside their burning encasement inside the kingdom of the damned, Farinata and Cavalcante are seen at a moment when we have "left the earthly sphere behind; we are in an eternal place, and yet we encounter concrete appearance and concrete occurrence there. This differs from what appears and occurs on earth, yet it is evidently con- nected with it in a necessary and determined relation" (191).

The result is "a tremendous concentration [in Dante's style and vision]. We behold an intensified image of the essence of their being, fixed for all eternity in gigantic dimensions, behold it in a purity and distinctness which could never for one moment have been possible during their lives on earth" (192). What fascinates Auerbach is the mounting tension within Dante's poem, as eternally condemned sinners press their cases and aspire to the realization of their ambitions even as they remain fixed in the place assigned to them by divine judgment. Hence, the sense of futility and sublimity exuded simultaneously by the *Inferno*'s "earthly historicity" which is always pointed in the end toward the white rose of the *Paradiso*. So then "the beyond is eternal and yet phenomenal . . . it is changeless and of all time and yet full of history" (197). For Auerbach, therefore, Dante's great poem exemplifies the figural approach, the past realized in the present, the present prefiguring as well as acting like a sort of eternal redemption, the whole thing witnessed by Dante the pilgrim, whose artistic genius compresses human drama into an aspect of the divine.

The refinement of Auerbach's own writing about Dante is truly exhilarating to read, not just because of his complex, paradox-filled insights but, as he nears the end of the chapter, because of their Nietzschean audacity, often venturing toward the unsayable and the inexpressible, beyond normal or for that matter even divinely set limits. Having established the systematic nature of Dante's universe (framed by Aquinas's theocratic cosmology), Auerbach offers the thought that for all of its investment in the eternal and immutable, the *Divine Comedy* is even more successful in representing reality as basically human. In that vast work of art, "the image of man eclipses the image of God" (202), and despite Dante's Christian conviction that the world is made coherent by a systematic universal order, "the indestructibility of the whole historical and individual man turns *against* that order, makes it subservient to its own purposes, and obscures it" (202). Auerbach's great predecessor Vico had flirted with the idea that the human mind creates the divine, not the other way round, but living under the Church's umbrella in eighteenth-century Naples, Vico wrapped his defiant proposition in all sorts of formulae that seemed to preserve history for divine Providence and not for human creativity and ingenuity. Auerbach's

choice of Dante for advancing the radically humanistic thesis
carefully works through the great poet's Catholic ontology as
a phase transcended by the Christian epic's realism, which is
shown to be "ontogenetic," that is, "we are given to see, in the
realm of timeless being, the history of man's inner life and
unfolding" (202).

Yet Dante's Christian and post-Christian achievement
couldn't have been realized had it not been for his immersion
in what he inherited from classical culture: the capacity to
draw human figures clearly, dramatically, and forcefully. In
Auerbach's view, Western literature after Dante draws on his
example, but it is rarely as intensely convincing in its variety,
its dramatic realism and stark universality as he was. Successive chapters of *Mimesis* treat medieval and early Renaissance
texts as departures from the Dantean norm, some of them,
such as Montaigne's *Essais*, stressing personal experience at
the expense of the symphonic whole, others, such as the
works of Shakespeare and Rabelais, brimming over with a
linguistic verve and resourcefulness that overwhelms realistic
representation in the interests of language itself. Characters
like Falstaff or Pantagruel are realistically drawn to a certain
degree, but what is as interesting to the reader as their vivid-
ness are the unprecedently riotous effects of the author's style.
It isn't a contradiction to say that this couldn't have happened
without the emergence of humanism, as well as the great
geographical discoveries of the period: both have the effect of
expanding the potential range of human action while also
continuing to ground it in earthly situations. Auerbach says
that Shakespeare's plays, for instance, adumbrate "a basic fabric of the world, perpetually weaving itself, renewing itself,
and connected in all its parts, from which all this arises and
which makes it impossible to isolate any one event or level of
style. Dante's general clearly delimited figurality, in which
everything is resolved in the beyond, in God's ultimate king-

dom, and in which all characters attain their full realization only in the beyond, is no more" (327).

From this point on, reality is completely historical and it, rather than the Beyond, has to be read and understood according to laws that evolve slowly. Figural interpretation took for its point of origin the sacred word, or Logos, whose incarnation in the earthly world was made possible by the Christ-figure, a central point, as it were, for organizing experience and understanding history. With the eclipse of the divine that is presaged in Dante's poem, a new order slowly begins to assert itself, and so the second half of *Mimesis* painstakingly traces the growth of historicism, a multiperspectival, dynamic, and holistic way of representing history and reality. Let me quote him at length on the subject:

> Basically, the way in which we view human life and society is the same whether we are concerned with things of the past or things of the present. A change in our manner of viewing history will of necessity soon be transferred to our manner of viewing current conditions. When people realize that epochs and societies are not to be judged in terms of a pattern concept of what is desirable absolutely speaking but rather in every case in terms of their own premises; when people reckon among such premises not only natural factors like climate and soil but also the intellectual and historical factors; when, in other words, they come to develop a sense of historical dynamics, of the incomparability of historical phenomena and of their constant inner mobility; when they come to appreciate the vital unity of individual epochs, so that each epoch appears as a whole whose character is reflected in each of its manifestations; when, finally, they accept the conviction that the meaning of events cannot be grasped in abstract and general forms of cognition and that the material needed to understand it must not be sought exclusively in the upper strata of society and in major political events but also in art, economy, material and intellectual culture, in the depths of the workaday world and its

men and women, because it is only there that one can grasp
what is unique, what is animated by inner forces, and what, in
both a more concrete and a more profound sense, is universally
valid: then it is to be expected that those insights will also be
transferred to the present and that, in consequence, the present
too will be seen as incomparable and unique, as animated by
inner forces and in a constant state of development; in other
words, as a piece of history whose everyday depths and total
inner structure lay claim to our interest both in their origins
and in the direction taken by their development. (443–44)

Auerbach never loses sight of his original ideas about the
separation and mingling of styles, how, for instance, classicism
in France returned to the vogue for antique models and the
high style, and late-eighteenth-century German romanticism
overturned those norms by way of a hostile reaction to them
in works of sentiment and passion. And yet in a rare moment
of severe judgment, Auerbach shows that far from using the
advantages of historicism to represent the complexity and
social change that were overtaking contemporary reality,
early-nineteenth-century German culture (with the exception of Marx) turned away from it out of a fear of the future,
which to Germany seemed always to be barging in at the culture from the outside in forms such as revolution, civil unrest,
and the overturning of tradition.

Goethe comes in for the harshest treatment, even though
we know that Auerbach loved his poetry and read him with
the greatest pleasure. I do not think it is reading too much into
the somewhat judgmental tone of chapter 17 of *Mimesis*
("Miller the Musician") to recognize that in its stern con-
demnation of Goethe's dislike of upheaval and even of change
itself, his interest in aristocratic culture, his deep-seated wish
to be rid of the "revolutionary occurrences" taking place all
over Europe, his inability to understand the flow of popular
history, Auerbach was discussing no mere failure of perception

but a profound wrong turn in German culture as a whole that led to the horrors of the present. Perhaps Goethe is made to represent too much. But were it not for his withdrawal from the present and for what he otherwise might have done for bringing German culture into the dynamic present, Auerbach speculates that Germany might have been integrated "into the emerging reality of Europe and the world might have been prepared more calmly, have been accomplished with fewer uncertainties and less violence" (452).

At the time these regretful and actually understated lines were being written in the early 1940s, Germany had unleashed a storm on Europe that swept all before it. Before that, the major German writers after Goethe were mired in regionalism and a marvelously traditional conception of life as a vocation. Realism never emerged in Germany, and, except for Fontane, there was very little in the language that had the gravity, universality, and synthetic power to represent modern reality until Thomas Mann's *Buddenbrooks* in 1901. There is a brief acknowledgment that Nietzsche and Burkhardt were more in touch with their own time, but neither of course was "concerned with the realistic portrayal of contemporary reality" (519). As against the chaotic irrationality ultimately represented by the anachronistic ethos of National Socialism, Auerbach therefore locates an alternative in the realism of mainly French prose fiction, in which writers such as Stendhal, Flaubert, and Proust sought to unify the fragmented modern world—with its unfolding class struggle, its industrialization, and its economic expansion combined with moral discomfort—in the eccentric structures of the modernist novel. And these replace the correspondence between Eternity and History that had enabled Dante's vision and which was now completely overtaken by the disruptive and dislocating currents of historical modernity.

The last few chapters of *Mimesis* thus seem to have a different tone than what goes before them. Auerbach is now dis-

cussing the history of his own time, not that of the medieval
and renaissance past nor that of relatively distant cultures.
Evolving slowly from acute observation of events and characters in the mid-nineteenth century, realism in France (and,
though he talks about it much less, England) takes on the character of an aesthetic style capable of rendering sordidness and
beauty with unadorned directness, although in the process
master-technicians like Flaubert also formulated an ethic of
disinterested observation, unwilling to intervene in the rapidly
changing world of social upheaval and revolutionary change.
It is enough to be able to see and represent what is going on,
although the practice of realism usually concerns figures from
low or, at most, bourgeois life. How this then turns into the
magnificent richness of Proust's work based on memory or into
the stream-of-consciousness techniques of Virginia Woolf and
James Joyce is a topic that makes for some of Auerbach's most
impressive later pages, though once again we should remind
ourselves that what Auerbach is also describing is how his own
work as a philologist emerges from modernity and is indeed
an integral part of the representation of reality. Thus the modern Romance philology exemplified by Auerbach acquires its
special intellectual identity by a kind of conscious affiliation
with the realistic literature of its own time: the uniquely
French achievement of dealing with reality from more than a
local standpoint, universally, and with a specifically European
mission. *Mimesis* bears within its pages its own rich history of
the analysis of evolving styles and perspectives.

To help one understand the cultural and personal significance of Auerbach's quest, I'd like to recall the laboriously
complicated narrative structure of Mann's postwar novel *Dr.
Faustus*, which far more explicitly than *Mimesis* (it was published after Auerbach's work) is a story both of modern German catastrophe as well as the attempt to understand it. The
terrible story of Adrien Leverkuhn, a prodigiously endowed

composer who makes a pact with the devil to explore the furthest reaches of art and mind, is narrated by his much less gifted childhood friend and companion, Serenus Zeitblom. Whereas Adrien's wordless musical domain allows him to enter the irrational and the purely symbolic on his way down into terminal madness, Zeitblom, who is a humanist and scholar, tries to keep up with him, translating Adrien's musical journey into sequential prose, struggling to make sense of what defies ordinary comprehension. Mann suggests that both men represent the two aspects of modern German culture, one as embodied in Leverkuhn's defiant life and his pathbreaking music, which takes him beyond ordinary sense into the irrational demonic, the other as delivered in Zeitblom's sometimes bumbling and awkward narrative, that of a closely connected friend witnessing that which he is powerless to stop or prevent.

The novel's fabric is actually made up of three strands. In addition to Adrien's story and Zeitblom's attempts to grapple with it (which include the story of Zeitblom's own life and career as a scholarly humanist and teacher), there are frequent allusions to the course of the war, concluding with Germany's final defeat in 1945. That history is not referred to in *Mimesis,* nor of course is there anything in it like the drama and the cast of characters that animates Mann's great novel. But in its allusions to the failure of German literature to confront modern reality and Auerbach's own effort in his book to represent an alternative history for Europe (Europe perceived through the means of stylistic analysis), *Mimesis* is also an attempt to rescue sense and meanings from the fragments of modernity with which, from his Turkish exile, Auerbach saw the downfall of Europe, and Germany's in particular. Like Zeitblom, he affirms the recuperative and redemptive human project for which, in its patient philological unfolding, his book is the emblem, and again resembling Zeitblom, he understands that like a novelist, the scholar must reconstruct the history of his own time as part of a personal commitment to his field. Yet Auerbach specifically forswears the linear narrative style that, despite its numerous interruptions and parentheses, works so powerfully for Zeitblom and his readers.

Thus in comparing himself to modern novelists, such as Joyce and Woolf, who re-create a whole world out of random, usually unimportant moments, Auerbach explicitly rejects a rigid scheme, a relentless sequential movement, or fixed concepts as instruments of study. "As opposed to this," he says near the end, "I see the possibility of success and profit in a method which consists in letting myself be guided by a few motifs which I have worked out gradually and without a specific purpose which have become vital and familiar to me in the course of my philological activity" (548). What gives him the confidence to surrender to those motifs without a specific purpose is, first, the realization that no one person can possibly synthesize the whole of modern life and, second, that there is an abiding "order and interpretation of life which arise from life itself; that is, those which grow up in the individuals themselves, which are to be discerned in their in their thoughts, their consciousness, and in a more concealed form in their words and actions. For there is always going on within us a process of formulation and interpretation whose subject matter is our own self" (549).

This testimonial to self-understanding is a deeply affecting one, I think. Several recognitions and affirmations are at play and even at odds within it, so to speak. One of course is staking something as ambitious as the history of Western representations of reality neither on a preexisting method nor a schematic time frame, but on personal interest, learning, and practice alone. Second, this then suggests that interpreting literature is "a process of formulation and interpretation whose subject matter is our own self." Third, rather than producing a totally coherent, neatly inclusive view of the subject, there is "not one order and one interpretation, but many, which may either be those of different persons or of the same person at different times; so that overlapping, complementing and contradiction yield something that we might call a synthesized cosmic view or at least a challenge to the reader's will to interpretive synthesis" (549).

Thus it all unmistakably comes down to a personal effort. Auerbach offers no system, no short cut to what he puts before us as a history of the representation of reality in Western literature. From a contemporary standpoint, there is something impossibly naïve, if not outrageous, that hotly contested terms like "Western," "reality," and "representation"—each of which has recently brought forth literally acres of disputatious prose from critics and philosophers—are left to stand on their own, unadorned and unqualified. It is as if Auerbach was intent on exposing his personal explorations and, perforce, his fallibility to the perhaps scornful eye of critics who might deride his subjectivity. But the triumph of *Mimesis*, as well as its inevitable tragic flaw, is that the human mind studying literary representations of the historical world can only do so as any author does, from the limited perspective of one's own time and one's own work. No more scientific a method and less a subjective a gaze is possible, except that the great scholar can always buttress his vision with learning, dedication, and moral purpose. It is this combination, this mingling of styles, out of which *Mimesis* emerges. And to my way of thinking, its humanistic example remains an unforgettable one, fifty years after its first appearance in English.

References

Auerbach, Erich. "Epilegomenon zu Minesis." *Romanische Forscungen* 65 (1953).

———. "Figura." In *Scenes From the Drama of European Literature*. Minneapolis: University of Minnesota Press, 1984.

———. *Dante: Poet of the Secular World*. Chicago: University of Chicago Press, 1961.

———. *Literary Language and Its Public in Late Latin Antiquity and in the Middle Ages*. Trans. Ralph Manheim. Princeton, N.J.: Princeton University Press, 1993.

———. *Mimesis: The Representation of Reality in Western Literature*. Trans. Willard R. Trask, intro. Edward Said. Princeton, N.J.: Princeton University Press, 2003.

———. "Philologie der Weltliteratur." Trans. Edward Said and Maire Said. *Centennial Review* 13 (1969).

Green, Geoffrey. *Literary Criticism and the Structures of History: Erich Auerbach and Leo Spitzer*. Lincoln: University of Nebraska Press, 1982.

Lowry, Nelson, Jr. "Erich Auerbach: Memoir of a Scholar." *Yale Review* 69, no. 2 (Winter 1980).

Vico, Giambattista. *The New Science of Giambattista Vico*. Trans. Thomas Goddard Bergin and Max Harold Fisch. Ithaca, N.Y.: Cornell University Press, 1984.

5

THE PUBLIC ROLE OF WRITERS AND INTELLECTUALS

IN 1981, *THE NATION* MAGAZINE CONVENED A CONGRESS OF writers in New York by putting out notices for the event and, as I understood the tactic, leaving open the question of who was a writer and why he or she qualified to attend. The result was that literally hundreds of people showed up, crowding the main ballroom of a midtown Manhattan hotel almost to the ceiling. The occasion itself was intended as a response by the intellectual and artistic communities to the immediate onset of the Reagan era. As I recall the proceedings, a debate raged for a long time over the definition of a writer in the hope that some of the people there would be selected out or, in plain English, forced to leave. The reason for that was twofold: first of all, to decide who had a vote and who didn't, and, second, to form a writer's union. Not much occurred in the way of reduced and manageable numbers; the hearteningly large mass of people simply remained immense and unwieldy since it was quite clear that everyone who came as a writer who opposed Reaganism stayed on as a writer who opposed Reaganism.

I remember clearly that at one point someone sensibly suggested that we should adopt what was said to be the Soviet position on defining a writer, that is, a writer is someone who says that he or she is a writer. And I think that is where matters seem to have rested, even though a National Writer's Union was formed but restricted its functions to technical professional matters such as fairer standardized contracts between publishers and writers. An American Writer's Congress to deal with expressly political issues was also formed, but it was derailed by people who in effect wanted it for one or another specific political agenda that could not get a consensus.

Since that time, an immense amount of change has taken place in the world of writers and intellectuals, and, if anything, the definition of who or what is a writer and intellectual has become more confusing and difficult to pin down. I tried my hand at it in my 1993 Reith Lectures, *Representations of the Intellectual*, but there have been major political and economic transformations since that time, and in writing this essay, I have found myself revising a great deal and adding to some of my earlier views. Central to these changes has been the deepening of an unresolved tension as to whether writers and intellectuals can ever be what is called nonpolitical, and, if so, how and in what measure. The difficulty of the tension for the individual writer and intellectual has been paradoxically that the realm of the political and public has expanded so much as to be virtually without borders. Consider that the bipolar world of the Cold War has been reconfigured and dissolved in several different ways, all of them first of all providing what seems to be an infinite number of variations on the location or position, physical and metaphorical, of the writer, and, secondly, opening up the possibility of divergent roles for him or her to play if, that is, the notion of writer or intellectual itself can be said to have any coherent and definably separate meaning or existence at all. The role of the American writer in the post-9/11 period has certainly amplified the pertinence of what is written about "us" to an enormous degree.

Yet, despite the spate of books and articles saying that intellectuals no longer exist and that the end of the Cold War, the opening up of the mainly American university to legions of writers and intellectuals, the age of specialization, and the commercialization and commodification of everything in the newly globalized economy have simply done away with the old somewhat romantic-heroic notion of the solitary writer-intellectual (I shall provisionally connect the two terms for purposes of convenience here, then go on to explain my reasons for doing so in a moment), there still seems to be a great deal of life in the ideas and practices of writer-intellectuals that touch on, and are very much a part of the public realm. Their role most recently in opposing (as well, alas, as supporting) the Anglo-American war in Iraq is very much a case in point.

In the three or four quite distinct contemporary language cultures that I know something about, the importance of writers and intellectuals is eminently, indeed overwhelmingly evident, in part because many people still feel the need to look at the writer-intellectual as someone who ought to be listened to as a guide to the confusing present, and also as a leader of a faction, tendency, or group vying for more power and influence. The Gramscian provenance of both these ideas about the role of an intellectual is clear.

Now, in the Arab-Islamic world, the two words used for intellectual are "*muthaqqaf*," and "*mufakir*," the first derived from "*thaqafa*," or culture (hence, a man of culture), the second from "*fikr*," or thought (hence, a man of thought). In both instances the prestige of those meanings is enhanced and amplified by implied comparison with government, which is now widely regarded as without credibility and popularity, or culture and thought. So in the moral vacancy created, for example, by dynastic republican governments like those of Egypt, Iraq, Libya, or Syria, many people turn either to religious or secular intellectuals (still predominantly male) for the leadership no longer provided by political authority, even though governments have been adept at co-opting intellectuals as mouthpieces for them. But the search for authentic intellectuals goes on, as does the struggle.

In the French-speaking domains, the word "*intellectuel*" unfailingly carries with it some residue of the public realm in which recently deceased figures like Sartre, Foucault, Bourdieu, and Aron debated and put forward their views for very large audiences indeed. By the early 1980s, when most of the *maîtres penseurs* had disappeared, a certain gloating and relief accompanied their absence, as if the new redundancy gave a lot of little people a chance to have their say for the first time since Zola. Today, with what seems like a revival of Sartre in evidence and with Pierre Bourdieu or his ideas appearing almost to the day of his death in every other issue of *Le Monde* and *Libération*, a considerably aroused taste for public intellectuals has gripped many people, I think. From a distance, debate about social and economic policy seems pretty lively, and isn't quite as one-sided as it is in the United States.

Raymond Williams's succinct presentation in *Keywords* of the force field of mostly negative connotations for the word "intellectual" is about as good a starting point for understanding the historical semantics of the word as has come out of England. Excellent subsequent work by Stefan Collini, John Carey, and others has considerably deepened and refined the field of practice where intellectuals and writers have been located. Williams himself has gone on to indicate that, after the middle of the twentieth century, the word takes on a new, somewhat wider set of associations, many of them having to do with ideology, cultural production, and the capacity for organized thought and learning. This suggests that English usage has expanded to take in some of the meanings and uses that have been quite common in the French and generally European contexts. But as in the French instance, intellectuals of Williams's generation have passed from the scene (the almost miraculously articulate and brilliant Eric Hobsbawm being a rare exception) and, to judge from some of his successors on the *New Left Review*, a new period of Leftist quietism may have set in. Especially given New Labour's thorough renunciation of its own past and its joining the new American campaign to reorder the world, there is a fresh opportunity to appreciate the dissenting role of the European writer. Neo-liberal and Thatcherite intellectuals are pretty much where they have been (in the ascendancy) and have the advantage of many more pulpits in the press from which to speak, for example, to support or criticize the war in Iraq.

In the American setting, however, the word "intellectual" is less used than in the three other arenas of discourse and discussion that I've mentioned. One reason is that professionalism and specialization provide the norm for intellectual work much more than they do in Arabic, French, or British English. The cult of expertise has never ruled the world of discourse as much as it now does in the United States, where the policy intellectual can feel that he or she surveys the entire world. Another reason is that even though the United States is actually full of intellectuals hard at work filling the airwaves, print and cyberspace with their effusions, the public realm is so taken up with questions of policy and government, as well as with considerations of power and authority, that even the idea of an intellectual who is driven neither by a passion for office nor by the ambition to get the ear of someone in power is difficult to sustain for more than a second or two. Profit and celebrity are powerful stimulants. In far too many years of appearing on television or being interviewed by journalists, I have never *not* been asked the question, "what do you think the United States should do about such and such an issue?" I take this to be an index of how the notion of rule has been lodged at the very heart of intellectual practice outside the university. And may I add that it has been a point of principle for me *not ever* to reply to the question.

Yet it is also overwhelmingly true that in America there is no shortage in the public realm of partisan policy intellectuals who are organically linked to one or another political party, lobby, special interest, or foreign power. The world of the Washington think tanks, the various television talk shows, innumerable radio programs, to say nothing of literally thousands of occasional papers, journals, and magazines—all this testifies amply to how densely saturated public discourse is with interests, authorities, and powers whose extent in the aggregate is literally unimaginable in scope and variety, except as that whole bears centrally on the acceptance of a neoliberal postwelfare state responsive neither to the citizenry nor to the natural environment, but to a vast structure of global corporations unrestricted by traditional barriers or sovereignties. The unparalleled global military reach of the United States is integral to the new structure. With the various specialized systems and practices of the new economic situation, only very gradually and partially being disclosed, and with an administration whose idea of national security is preemptive war, we are beginning to discern an immense panorama of how these systems and practices (many of them new, many of them refashioned holdovers from the classical imperial system) have been assembled to provide a geography whose purpose is slowly to crowd out and override human agency. (See, as an instance of what I have in mind, Yves Dezelay and Bryant G. Garth, *Dealing in Virtue: International Commercial Arbitration and the Con-*

struction of a Transnational Legal Order). We must not be misled by the effusions of Thomas Friedman, Daniel Yergin, Joseph Stanislas, and the legions who have celebrated globalization into believing that the system itself is the best outcome for human history, nor in reaction should we fail to note what in a far less glamorous way globalization from below, as Richard Falk has called the post-Westphalian world-system, can provide by way of human potential and innovation. There is now a fairly extensive network of NGOs created to address minority and human rights, women's and environmental issues, and movements for democratic and cultural change, and while none of these can be a substitute for political action or mobilization, especially to protest and try to prevent illegal wars, many of them do embody resistance to the advancing global status quo.

Yet, as Dezelay and Garth have argued ("L'impérialisme de la vertu"), given the funding of many of these international NGOs, they are co-optable as targets by what the two researchers have called the imperialism of virtue, functioning as annexes to the multinationals and great foundations like Ford, the centers of civic virtue that forestall deeper kinds of change or critiques of longstanding assumptions.

In the meantime, it is sobering and almost terrifying to contrast the world of academic intellectual discourse, in its generally hermetic, jargon-ridden, unthreatening combativeness, with what the public realm all around has been doing. Masao Miyoshi has pioneered the study of this contrast, especially in its marginalization of the humanities. The separation between the two realms, academic and public, is, I think, greater in the United States than anywhere else, although in Perry Anderson's dirge for the Left with which he announces his editorship of *New Left Review*, it is all too plain that in his opinion the British, American, and Continental pantheon of remaining heroes is, with one exception, resolutely, exclusively academic and almost entirely male and Eurocentric. I found it extraordinary that he takes no account of nonacademic intellectuals like John Pilger and Alexander Cockburn, or major academic and political figures such as Chomsky, Zinn, the late Eqbal Ahmad, Germaine Greer, or such diverse figures as Mohammed Sid Ahmad, bell hooks, Angela Davis, Cornel West, Serge Halimi, Miyoshi, Ranajit Guha, Partha Chatterjee, to say nothing of an impressive battery of Irish intellectuals that would include Seamus Deane, Luke Gibbons, Declan Kiberd, plus many others, all of whom would certainly not accept the solemn lament intoned for what he calls the "the neo-liberal grand slam."

The great novelty alone of Ralph Nader's candidacy in the 2000 American presidential campaign was that a genuine adversarial intellectual was running for the most powerful elected office in the world using the rhetoric and tactics of demystification and disenchantment, in the process supplying a mostly disaffected electorate with alternative information buttressed with precise facts and figures. This went completely against the prevailing modes of vagueness, vapid slogans, mystification, and religious fervor sponsored by the two major party candidates, underwritten by the media and, paradoxically by virtue of its inaction, the humanistic academy. Nader's competitive stance was a sure sign of how far from over and defeated the oppositional tendencies in global society are; witness also the upsurge of reformism in Iran, the consolidation of democratic antiracism in various parts of Africa, and so on, leaving aside the November 1999 action in Seattle against the WTO, the liberation of South Lebanon, the unprecedented worldwide protests against war in Iraq, and so on. The list would be a long one and very different in tone (were it to be interpreted fully) from the consolatory accomodationism Anderson seems to recommend. In intention, Nader's campaign was also different from those of his opponents in that he aimed to arouse the citizenry's democratic awareness of the untapped potential for participation in the country's resources, not just greed or simple assent to what passes for politics.

Having summarily assimilated the words intellectual and writer to each other a moment ago, it is best for me now to show why and how they belong together, despite the writer's separate origin and history. In the language of everyday use, a writer, in the languages and cultures that I am familiar with, is a person who produces literature, that is, a novelist, a poet, a dramatist. I think it is generally true that in all cultures writers have a separate, perhaps even more honorific, place than do intellectuals; the aura of creativity and an almost sanctified capacity for originality (often vatic in its scope and quality) accrues to them as it does not at all to intellectuals, who, with regard to literature, belong to the slightly debased and parasitic class of critics. (There is a long history of attacks on critics as nasty, niggling beasts capable of little more than carping and pedantic word-mongering). Yet during the last years of the twentieth century, the writer has taken on more and more of the intellectual's adversarial attributes in such activities as speaking the truth to power, being a witness to persecution and suffering, and supplying a dissenting voice in conflicts with authority. Signs of the amalgamation of one to the other would have to include the Salman Rushdie case in all its ramifications, the formation of numerous writers' parliaments and congresses devoted to such issues as intolerance, the dialogue of cultures, civil strife (as in Bosnia and Algeria), freedom of speech and censorship, truth and reconciliation (as in South Africa, Argentina, Ireland, and elsewhere), and the special symbolic role of the writer as an intellectual testifying to a country's or region's experience, thereby giving that experience a public identity forever inscribed in the global discursive agenda. The easiest way of demonstrating this dovetailing is simply to list the names of some (but by no means all) recent Nobel Prize winners, then to allow each name to trigger in the mind an emblematized region, which in turn can be seen as a sort of platform or jumping-off point for that writer's subsequent activity as an intervention in debates taking place very far from the world of literature: thus, Nadine Gordimer, Kenzaburo Oe, Derek Walcott, Wole Soyinka, Gabriel García Márquez, Octavio Paz, Elie Wiesel, Bertrand Russell, Gunter Grass, and Rigoberta Menchu, among several others.

Now it is also true, as Pascal Casanova has brilliantly shown in her synoptic book *La république mondiale des lettres*, that, fashioned over the past 150 years, there now seems to be a global system of literature in place, complete with its own order of literariness (*litterarité*), tempo, canon, internationalism, and market values. The efficiency of the system is that it seems to have generated the types of writers that she discusses as belonging to such different categories as assimilated, dissident, translated figures, all of them both individualized and classified in what she clearly shows is a highly efficient, globalized, quasi-market system. The drift of her argument is in effect to show how this powerful and all-pervasive system can even go as far as to stimulate a kind of independence from it, in cases like those of Joyce and Beckett, writers whose language and orthography do not submit to the laws either of state or of system.

Much as I admire it, however, the overall achievement of Casanova's book is nevertheless contradictory. She seems to be saying that literature as a globalized system has a kind of integral autonomy to it that places it in large measure just beyond the gross realities of political institutions and discourse, a notion that has a certain theoretical plausibility to it when she puts it in the form of "*un espace littéraire internationale*," with its own laws of interpretation, its own dialectic of individual work and ensemble, its own problematics of nationalism and national languages. But she doesn't go as far as Adorno in saying, as I would too (and plan to return to briefly at the end), that one of the hallmarks of modernity is how at a very deep level, the aesthetic and the social need to be kept, and are often consciously kept, in a state of irreconcilable tension. Nor does she spend enough time discussing the ways in which the literary, or the writer, is still implicated in, indeed frequently mobilized for use in, the great post–Cold War cultural contests provided by the altered political configurations I spoke of earlier.

In that wider setting, then, the basic distinction between writers and intellectuals need not be made since, insofar as they both act in the new public sphere dominated by globalization (and assumed to exist even by adherents of the Khomeini fatwa), their public role as writers and intellectuals can be discussed and analyzed together. Another way of putting it is to say that I shall be concentrating on what writers and intellectuals have in common as they intervene in the public sphere. I don't at all want to give up the possibility that there remains an area outside and untouched by the globalized one that I shall be discussing here, but I don't want to discuss this until the end of the essay, since my main concern is with the writer's role squarely within the actually existing system.

Let me say something about the technical characteristics of intellectual intervention today. To get a dramatically vivid grasp of the speed to which communication has accelerated during the past decade, I'd like to contrast Jonathan Swift's awareness of effective public intervention in the early eighteenth cenury with ours. Swift was surely the most devastating pamphleteer of his time, and during his campaign against the Duke of Marlborough in 1713 and 1714, he was able to get 15,000 copies of his pamphlet "The Conduct of the Allies" onto the streets in a few days. This brought down the Duke from his high eminence but nevertheless did not change Swift's pessimistic impression (dating back to *A Tale of a Tub*, 1694) that his writing was basically temporary, good only for the short time that it circulated. He had in mind of course the running quarrel between ancients and moderns in which venerable writers like Homer and Horace had the advantage of great longevity, even permanence, over modern figures like Dryden by virtue of their age and the authenticity of their views. In the age of electronic media, such considerations are mostly irrelevant, since anyone with a computer and decent Internet access is capable of reaching numbers of people thousands of times greater than Swift did, and can also look forward to the preservation of what is written beyond any conceivable measure. Our ideas today of archive and discourse must be radically modified and can no longer be defined as Foucault painstakingly tried to describe them a mere two decades ago. Even if one writes for a newspaper or journal, the chances of multiplying reproduction and, notionally at least, an unlimited time of preservation have wrought havoc on even the idea of an actual, as opposed to a virtual, audience. These things have certainly limited the powers that regimes have to censor or ban writing that is considered dangerous, although, as I shall note presently, there are fairly crude means for stopping or curtailing the libertarian function of on-line print. Until only very recently, Saudi Arabia and Syria, for example, successfully banned the Internet and even satellite television. Both countries now tolerate limited access to the Internet, although both have also installed sophisticated and, in the long run, prohibitively interdictory processes to maintain their control.

As things stand, an article I might write in New York for a British paper has a good chance of reappearing on individual Web sites or via e-mail on screens in the United States, Europe, Japan, Pakistan, the Middle East, Latin America, and South Africa, as well as Australia. Authors and publishers have very little control over what is reprinted and recirculated. For whom then does one write, if it is difficult to specify the audience with any sort of precision? Most people, I think, focus on the actual outlet that has commissioned the piece or on the putative readers we would like to address. The idea of an imagined community has suddenly acquired a very literal, if virtual, dimension. Certainly, as I experienced when I began more than ten years ago to write in an Arabic publication for an audience of Arabs, one attempts to create, shape, refer to a constituency, much more now than during Swift's time, when he could quite naturally assume that the persona he called a Church of England man was in fact his real, very stable, and quite small audience.

All of us should therefore operate today with some notion of very probably reaching much larger audiences than any we could have conceived of even a decade ago, although the chances of retaining that audience are by the same token quite small. This is not simply a matter of optimism of the will; it is in the very nature of writing today. This makes it very difficult for writers to take common assumptions between them and their audiences for granted or to assume that references and allusions are going to be understood immediately. But, writing in this expanded new space strangely does have a further unusually risky consequence, which is that it is easy to be encouraged to say things that are either completely opaque or completely transparent, and if one has any sense of the intellectual and political vocation (which I shall get to in a moment), it should of course be the latter rather than the former. But then, transparent, simple, clear prose presents its own challenges, since the ever present danger is that one can fall into the misleadingly simple neutrality of a journalistic World-English idiom that is indistinguishable from CNN or *USA Today* prose. The quandary is a real one, whether in the end to repel readers (and more dangerously, meddling editors) or to attempt to win readers over in a style that perhaps too closely resembles the mind-set one is trying to expose and challenge. The thing to remember, I keep telling myself, is that there isn't another language at hand, that the language I use must be the same used by the State Department or the president when they say that they are for human rights and for fighting a war to "liberate" Iraq, and I must be able to use that very same language to recapture the subject, reclaim it, and reconnect it to the tremendously complicated realities these vastly overprivileged antagonists of mine have simplified, betrayed, and either diminished or dissolved. It should be obvious by now that for an intellectual who is not there simply to advance someone else's interest, there have to be opponents that are held responsible for the present state of affairs, antagonists with whom one must directly engage.

While it is true and even discouraging that all the main outlets are, however, controlled by the most powerful interests and consequently by the very antagonists one resists or attacks, it is also true that a relatively mobile intellectual energy can take advantage of and, in effect, multiply the kinds of platforms available for use. On one side, therefore, six enormous multinationals presided over by six men control most of the world's supply of images and news. On the other, there are the independent intellectuals who actually form an incipient community, physically separated from each other but connected variously to a great number of activist communities shunned by the main media, and who have at their actual disposal other kinds of what Swift sarcastically called oratorical machines. Think of the impressive range of opportunities offered by the lecture platform, the pamphlet, radio, alternative journals, occasional papers, the interview, the rally, the church pulpit, and the Internet, to name only a few. True, it is a considerable disadvantage to realize that one is unlikely to get asked on to PBS's *NewsHour* or ABC's *Nightline* or, if one is in fact asked, only an isolated fugitive minute will be offered. But then, other occasions present themselves, not in the sound-bite format, but rather in more extended stretches of time. So rapidity is a double-edged weapon. There is the rapidity of the sloganeeringly reductive style that is the main feature of expert discourse—to-the-point, fast, formulaic, pragmatic in appearance—and there is the rapidity of response and format that intellectuals and indeed most citizens can exploit in order to present fuller, more complete expressions of an alternative point of view. I am suggesting that by taking advantage of what is available in the form of numerous platforms (or stages-itinerant, another Swiftian term) and an alert and creative willingness to exploit them by an intellectual (that is, platforms that either aren't available to or are shunned by the television personality, expert, or political candidate), it is possible to initiate wider discussion.

The emancipatory potential—and the threats to it—of this new situation mustn't be underestimated. Let me give a very powerful recent example of what I mean. There are about four million Palestinian refugees scattered all over the world, a significant number of whom live in large refugee camps in Lebanon (where the 1982 Sabra and Shatila massacres took place), Jordan, Syria, and in Israeli-occupied Gaza and the West Bank. In 1999, an enterprising group of young and educated refugees living in Deheisheh Camp, near Bethlehem on the West Bank, established the Ibdaa Center, whose main feature was the Across Borders project; this was a revolutionary way of connecting refugees in most of the main camps—separated geographically and politically by impossible, difficult barriers—to each other through computer terminals. For the first time since their parents were dispersed in 1948, second-generation Palestinian refugees in Beirut or Amman could communicate with their counterparts inside

Palestine. Some of what the participants in the project did was quite remarkable. Thus the Deheisheh residents went on visits to their former villages in Palestine and then described their emotions and what they saw for the benefit of other refugees who had heard of, but could not have access to, these places. In a matter of weeks, a remarkable solidarity emerged at a time, it turned out, when the ill-fated final-status negotiations between the PLO and Israel were beginning to take up the question of refugees and return, which along with the question of Jerusalem made up the intransigent core of the stalemated peace process. For some Palestinian refugees, therefore, their presence and political will was actualized for the first time, giving them a new status qualitatively different from the passive objecthood that had been their fate for half a century. On 26 August 2000, all the computers in Deheisheh were destroyed in an act of political vandalism that left no one in doubt that refugees were meant to remain as refugees, which is to say that they were not meant to disturb the status quo that had assumed their silence for so long. It wouldn't be hard to list the possible suspects, but it is hard to imagine that anyone will either be named or apprehended. In any case, the Deheisheh camp dwellers immediately set about trying to restore the Ibdaa Center, and they seem to some degree to have succeeded in so doing.

To answer the question of why, in this and other similar contexts, individuals and groups prefer writing and speaking to silence, is equivalent to specifying what the intellectual and writer confront in the public sphere. What I mean is that the existence of individuals or groups seeking social justice and economic equality, who understand (in Amartya Sen's formulation) that freedom must include the right to a whole range of choices affording cultural, political, intellectual, and economic development, ipso facto will lead one to a desire for articulation as opposed to silence. This is the functional idiom of the intellectual vocation. The intellectual therefore stands in a position to make possible and further the formulation of these expectations and wishes.

Now every discursive intervention is, of course, specific to a particular occasion and assumes an existing consensus, paradigm, episteme, or praxis (we can all pick our favorite concept that denotes the prevailing accepted discursive norm), say, during the Anglo-American war against Iraq, during national elections in Egypt and the United States, about immigration practices in one or another country, or about the ecology of West Africa. In each of these and so many other situations, the hallmark of the era we live in is that there tends to be a mainstream media–government orthodoxy against which it is very difficult indeed to go, even though the intellectual must assume that alternatives can clearly be shown to exist. Thus, to restate the obvious, every situation should be interpreted according to its own givens, but (and I would argue that this is almost always the case) every situation also contains a contest between a powerful system of interests, on the one hand, and, on the other, less powerful interests threatened with frustration, silence, incorporation, or extinction by the powerful. It almost goes without saying that for the American intellectual the responsibility is greater, the openings numerous, the challenge very difficult. The United States, after all, is the only global power; it intervenes nearly everywhere; and its resources for domination are very great, although very far from infinite.

The intellectual's role is dialectically, oppositionally to uncover and elucidate the contest I referred to earlier, to challenge and defeat both an imposed silence and the normalized quiet of unseen power wherever and whenever possible. For there is a social and intellectual equivalence between this mass of overbearing collective interests and the discourse used to justify, disguise, or mystify its workings while also preventing objections or challenges to it.

Pierre Bourdieu and his associates produced a collective work in 1993 entitled *La misère du monde* (translated in 1999 as *The Weight of the World: Social Suffering in Contemporary Society*), whose aim was to compel the politicians' attention to what, in French society, the misleading optimism of public discourse had hidden. This kind of book, therefore, plays a sort of negative intellectual role, whose aim is, to quote Bourdieu, "to produce and disseminate instruments of defense against symbolic domination which increasingly relies on the authority of science" or expertise or appeals to national unity, pride, history, and tradition, to bludgeon people into submission. Obviously India and Brazil are different from Britain and the United States, but those often striking disparities in cultures and economies shouldn't at all obscure the even more startling similarities that can be seen in some of the techniques and, very often, the aim of deprivation and repression that compel people to follow along meekly. I should also like to add that one needn't always present an abstruse and detailed theory of justice to go to war intellectually against injustice, since there is now a well-stocked internationalist storehouse of conventions, protocols, resolutions, and charters for national authorities to comply with, if they are so inclined. And, in the same context, I reject the ultrapostmodern position (like that taken by Richard Rorty while shadowboxing with some vague thing he refers to contemptuously as "the academic Left"), which holds, when confronting ethnic cleansing or genocide as was occurring in Iraq under the sanctions-regime or any of the evils of torture, censorship, famine, and ignorance (most of them constructed by humans, not by acts of God), that human rights are cultural or grammatical things, and when they are violated, they do not really have the status accorded them by crude foundationalists, such as myself, for whom they are as real as anything we can encounter.

I think it is correct to say that depoliticized or aestheticized submission, along with all of the different forms of, in some cases, triumphalism and xenophobia, in others, apathy and defeat, have been principally required since the 1960s to allay whatever residual feelings of desire for democratic participation (also known as "a danger to stability") still existed. One can read this plainly enough in *The Crisis of Democracy*, coauthored at the behest of the Trilateral Commission a decade before the end of the Cold War. There the argument is that too much democracy is bad for governability, which is that supply of passivity which makes it easier for oligarchies of technical or policy experts to push people into line. So if one is endlessly lectured by certified experts who explain that the freedom we all want demands deregulation and privatization or war and that the new world order is nothing less than the end of history, there is very little inclination to address this order with anything like individual or even collective demands. Chomsky has relentlessly addressed this paralyzing syndrome for several years.

Let me give an example from personal experience in the United States today of how formidable are the challenges to the individual and how easy it is to slip into inaction. If you are seriously ill, you are suddenly plunged into the world of outrageously expensive pharmaceutical products, many of which are still experimental and require FDA approval. Even those that aren't experimental and aren't particularly new (like steroids and antibiotics) are lifesavers, but their exorbitant expense is thought to be a small price to pay for their efficacy. The more one looks into the matter, the more one encounters the corporate rationale, which is that while the cost of manufacturing the drug may be small (it usually is tiny), the cost of research is enormous and must be recovered in subsequent sales. Then you discover that most of the research cost came to the corporation in the form of government grants, which in turn came from the taxes paid by every citizen. When you address the abuse of public money in the form of questions put to a promising, progressively minded candidate (e.g., Bill Bradley), you then quickly understand why such candidates never raise the question. They receive enormous campaign contributions from Merck and Bristol Meyers and are most unlikely to challenge their supporters. So you go on paying and living, on the assumption that if you are lucky enough to have an insurance policy, the insurance company will pay out. Then you discover that insurance company accountants make the decisions on who gets a costly medication or test, what is allowed or disallowed, for how long and in what circumstances, and only then do you understand that such rudimentary protections as a patient's genuine bill of rights still cannot be passed in Congress, given that immensely profitable insurance corporations lobby there indefatigably.

In short, I find myself saying that even heroic attempts (such as Fredric Jameson's) to understand the system on a theoretical level or to formulate what Samir Amin has called delinking alternatives are fatally undermined by their relative neglect of actual political intervention in the existential situations in which as citizens we find ourselves—intervention that isn't just personal but is a significant part of a broad adversarial or oppositional movement. Obviously, as intellectuals, we all carry around some working understanding or sketch of the global system (in large measure thanks to world and regional historians like Immanuel Wallerstein, Anwar Abdel Malek, J. M. Blaut, Janet Abu-Lughod, Peter Gran, Ali Mazrui, William McNeil), but it is during the direct encounters with it in one or another specific geography, configuration, or problematic that the contests are waged and perhaps even winnable. There is an admirable chronicle of the kind of thing I mean in the various essays of Bruce Robbins's *Feeling*

Global: Internationalism in Distress (1999), Timothy Brennan's *At Home in the World: Cosmopolitanism Now* (1997), and Neil Lazarus's *Nationalism and Cultural Practice in the Postcolonial World* (1999), books whose self-consciously territorial and highly interwoven textures are in fact an adumbration of the critical (and combative) intellectual's sense of the world we live in today, taken as episodes or even fragments of a broader picture that their work, as well as the work of others like them, is in the process of compiling. What they suggest is a map of experiences that would have been indiscernible, perhaps invisible two decades ago, but that in the aftermath of the classical empires, the end of the Cold War, the crumbling of the socialist and nonaligned blocks, the emergent dialectics between North and South in the era of globalization, cannot be excluded either from cultural study or from the precincts of the humanistic disciplines.

I've mentioned a few names not just to indicate how significant I think their contributions have been, but also to use them in order to leapfrog directly into some concrete areas of collective concern where, to quote Bourdieu for the last time, there is the possibility of "collective invention." He continues by saying that

> the whole edifice of critical thought is thus in need of critical reconstruction. This work of reconstruction cannot be done, as some thought in the past, by a single great intellectual, a master-thinker endowed with the sole resources of his singular thought, or by the authorized spokesperson for a group or an institution presumed to speak in the name of those without voice, union, party, and so on. This is where the collective intellectual [Bourdieu's name for individuals the sum of whose research and participation on common subjects constitutes a sort of ad hoc collective] can play its irreplaceable role, by helping to create the social conditions for the collective production of realist utopias.

My response to this is to stress the absence of any master plan or blueprint or grand theory for what intellectuals can do and the absence now of any utopian teleology toward which human history can be described as moving. Therefore one *invents* goals abductively—in the literal use of the Latin word "*inventio*" employed by rhetoricians to stress finding again, or reassembling from past performances, as opposed to the romantic use of invention as something you create from scratch. That is, one hypothesizes a better situation from the known historical and social facts. So, in effect, this enables intellectual performances on many fronts, in many places, many styles that keep in play both the sense of opposition and the sense of engaged participation that I mentioned a moment ago. Therefore, film, photography, and even music, along with all the arts of writing can be aspects of this activity. Part of what we do as intellectuals is not only to define the situation, but also to discern the possibilities for active intervention, whether we then perform them ourselves or acknowledge them in others who have either gone before or are already at work, the intellectual as lookout. Provincialism of the old kind—for example, a literary specialist whose field is early-seventeenth-century England—rules itself out and, quite frankly, seems uninteresting and needlessly neutered. The assumption has to be that even though one can't do or know about everything, it must always be possible not only to discern the elements of a struggle or tension or problem near at hand that can be elucidated dialectically, but also to sense that other people have a similar stake and work in a common project. I have found a brilliantly inspiring parallel for what I mean in Adam Phillips's recent book *Darwin's Worms*, in which Darwin's lifelong attention to the lowly earthworm revealed its capacity for expressing nature's variability and design without necessarily seeing the whole of either one or the other, thereby, in his work on earthworms, replacing "a creation myth with a secular maintenance myth" (Phillips, 46).

Is there some nontrivial way of generalizing about where and in what form such struggles are taking place now? I shall limit myself to saying a little about only three of these struggles, all of which are profoundly amenable to intellectual intervention and elaboration. The first is to protect against and forestall the disappearance of the past, which, in the rapidity of change, the reformulation of tradition, and the construction of simplified bowdlerizations of history, is at the very heart of the contest described by Benjamin Barber rather too sweepingly as "Jihad versus McWorld." The intellectual's role is to present alternative narratives and other perspectives on history than those provided by combatants on behalf of official memory and national identity and mission. At least since Nietzsche, the writing of history and the accumulations of memory have been regarded in many ways as one of the essential foundations of power, guiding its strategies, charting its progress. Look, for example, at the appalling exploitation of past suffering described in their accounts of the uses of the Holocaust by Tom Segev, Peter Novick, and Norman Finkelstein or, just to stay within the area of historical restitution and reparation, the invidious disfiguring, dismembering, and disremembering of significant historical experiences that do not have powerful enough lobbies in the present and therefore merit dismissal or belittlement. The need now is for deintoxicated, sober histories that make evident the multiplicity and complexity of history without allowing one to conclude that it moves forward impersonally, according to laws determined either by the divine or by the powerful.

The second struggle is to construct fields of coexistence rather than fields of battle as the outcome of intellectual labor. There are great lessons to be learned from decolonization, which are that, noble as its liberatory aims were, it did not often enough prevent the emergence of repressive nationalist replacements for colonial regimes, and that the process itself was almost immediately captured by the Cold War, despite the nonaligned movement's rhetorical efforts. What's more, it has been miniaturized and even trivialized by a small academic industry that has simply turned it into an ambiguous contest between ambivalent opponents. In the various contests over justice and human rights that so many of us feel we have joined, there needs to be a component to our engagement that stresses the need for the redistribution of resources and that advocates the theoretical imperative against the huge accumulations of power and capital that so distort human life.

Peace cannot exist without equality; this is an intellectual value desperately in need of reiteration, demonstration, and reinforcement. The seduction of the word itself—peace—is that it is surrounded by, indeed drenched in, the blandishments of approval, uncontroversial eulogizing, sentimental endorsement. The international media (as has been the case recently with the unsanctioned war in Iraq) uncritically amplifies, ornaments, and unquestioningly transmits all this to vast audiences for whom peace and war are spectacles for delectation and immediate consumption. It takes a good deal more courage, work, and knowledge to dissolve words like "war" and "peace" into their elements, recovering what has been left out of peace processes that have been determined by the powerful, and then placing that missing actuality back in the center of things, than it does to write prescriptive articles for "liberals," à la Michael Ignatieff, that urge more destruction and death for distant civilians under the banner of benign imperialism. The intellectual is perhaps a kind of countermemory, with its own counterdiscourse that will not allow conscience to look away or fall asleep. The best corrective, as Dr. Johnson said, is to imagine the person whom you are discussing—in this case the person on whom the bombs will fall—reading you in your presence.

Still, just as history is never over or complete, it is also the case that some dialectical oppositions are not reconcilable, not transcendable, not really capable of being folded into a sort of higher, undoubtedly nobler synthesis. My third example, and the one closest to home for me, is the struggle over Palestine, which, I have always believed, cannot really be simply resolved by a technical and ultimately janitorial rearrangement of geography allowing dispossessed Palestinians the right (such as it is) to live in about 20 percent of their land, which would be encircled and totally dependent on Israel. Nor, on the other hand would it be morally acceptable to demand that the Israelis should retreat from the whole of former Palestine, now Israel, becoming refugees like Palestinians all over again. No matter how I have searched for a resolution to this impasse, I cannot find one, for this is not a facile case of right versus right. It cannot be right ever to deprive an entire people of their land and heritage. The Jews too are what I have called a community of suffering and have brought with them a heritage of great tragedy. But unlike the Israeli sociologist Zeev Sternhell, who once made the point in my presence, I cannot agree that the conquest of Palestine was a necessary one. The notion offends the sense of real Palestinian pain, in its own way, also tragic.

Overlapping yet irreconcilable experiences demand from the intellectual the courage to say that *that* is what is before us, in almost exactly the way Adorno has throughout his work on music insisted that modern music can never be reconciled with the society that produced it, but in its intensely and often despairingly crafted form and content, music can act as a silent witness to the inhumanity all around. Any assimilation of individual musical work to its social setting is, says Adorno, false. I conclude with the thought that the intellectual's provisional home is the domain of an exigent, resistant, intransigent art into which, alas, one can neither retreat nor search for solutions. But only in that precarious exilic realm can one first truly grasp the difficulty of what cannot be grasped and then go forth to try anyway.

References

Bourdieu, Pierre. *The Weight of the World: Social Suffering in Contemporary Society*. Cambridge: Polity Press, 1999.

Brennan, Timothy. *At Home in the World: Cosmopolitanism Now*. Cambridge, Mass.: Harvard University Press, 1997.

Casanova, Pascal. *La republique mondiale des lettres*. Paris: Seuil, 1999.

Crozier, Michel, Samuel P. Huntington, and Joji Watanuki. *The Crisis of Democracy*. New York: New York University Press, 1975.

Dezelay, Yves, and Bryant G, Garth. *Dealing in Virtue: International Commercial Arbitration and the Construction of a Transnational Legal Order*. Chicago: University of Chicago Press, 1996.

——. "L'impérialisme de la vertu." *Le monde diplomatique* (May 2000). Available from http://www.monde-diplomatique.fr/2000/05/.

Lazarus, Neil. *Nationalism and Cultural Practice in the Postcolonial World*. New York: Cambridge Univeristy Press, 1999.

Phillips, Adam. *Darwin's Worms*. New York: Basic Books, 2000.

Robbins, Bruce. *Feeling Global: Internationalism in Distress*. New York: NYU Press, 1999.

Williams, Raymond. *A Vocabulary of Culture and Society*. New York: Oxford University Press, 1976.

INDEX